Learn To
LEAD
Effectively

33 **Essential Lessons On Guiding Your Team To Success**

Entrepreneur.  QUICK GUIDE

Learn To
LEAD
Effectively

33 Essential Lessons On Guiding Your Team To Success

BY THE STAFF OF ENTREPRENEUR MEDIA
AND ERIC BUTOW

Entrepreneur Press, Publisher
Cover Design: Andrew Welyczko
Production and Composition: Alan Barnett Design

This publication is designed to provide accurate and authoritative
information in regard to the subject matter covered. It is sold with the
understanding that the publisher is not engaged in rendering legal,
accounting, or other professional services. If legal advice or other expert
assistance is required, the services of a competent professional person should
be sought.

Library of Congress Cataloging-in-Publication Data
    Names: Butow, Eric, author. | Entrepreneur Press, issuing body.
    Title: Learn to lead effectively : 33 essential lessons on guiding your
        team to success / The Staff of Entrepreneur Media and Eric Butow.
    Description: Santa Ana, CA : Entrepreneur Press, [2025] |
        Includes index. |
        Summary: "Thirty-three game-changing lessons curated by real
        leadership experts to help you become a more effective
        leader"— Provided by publisher.
    Identifiers: LCCN 2024031191 (print) | LCCN 2024031192
        (ebook) | ISBN 9781642011784 (paperback) | ISBN
        9781613084885 (epub)
    Subjects: LCSH: Leadership. | Teams in the workplace.
    Classification: LCC HD57.7 .B879 2025 (print) | LCC HD57.7
        (ebook) | DDC 658.4/092—dc23/eng/20240709
    LC record available at https://lccn.loc.gov/2024031191
    LC ebook record available at https://lccn.loc.gov/2024031192

Contents

Contents

PART II
THE WHAT OF LEADERSHIP

Contents

Contents

PART III
THE HOW OF LEADERSHIP

Contents

Contents

Introduction

by Eric Butow

What makes a good leader? Some think all they must do is pick up a leadership book like this one to get the magic beans that will grow the beanstalk and raise your team and business to new heights. But we can tell that you didn't fall for it, because you already know that it takes hard work and dedication; just as with mastering any other craft. In John F. Kennedy's words, you understand that "leadership and learning are indispensable to each other."

This book is here to help you learn from people who have been gracious enough to share their experiences with Entrepreneur Media, because you need realistic insights and experiences that can inform you about how to lead your business and team members. By now, you've likely experienced a bad leader in your own career or, worse, had an absentee leader who said that you were doing a great job when the entire company was in disarray. (This brings to mind the cartoon with the dog drinking coffee in the flaming kitchen saying, "This is fine.")

Leadership is a people skill, and each person in your business brings their own culture, background, and personal experiences to your company. It is your job to bring them together

1

into one company culture, no matter if you're running a mom-and-pop store on Main Street or a multinational company. What's more, you need to keep your team focused on building the company into a successful business beyond anyone's wildest dreams.

If you are a manager in a large organization, you may not feel like you get any praise or even credit from anyone. Managers need to juggle three bowling balls in the air: their employees, the higher ups such as executives and owners, and customers who usually demand to talk to a manager when they are not satisfied with an employee's service. Oh, and you are supposed to whistle while you're at it.

If you find yourself nodding your head, keep in mind that when you effectively lead as the manager, you're more than just a taskmaster; you see the vision of the owner(s) and translate it into a purpose that your team members can get behind. Yes, you still need to keep a close eye on the metrics such as ROI that helps inform you on how your team members are doing. But you also need to be a human being each day by incorporating good communication skills, listening well, being patient when you deal with team members, resolving crisis situations, having difficult conversations, and empowering your team. It's all good when things are going well, but keep in mind what VaynerMedia CEO and social media star Gary Vaynerchuk observed: "When somebody screws up, that's when leadership really kicks in. When the money is flowing, when customers are happy, then everyone is a good leader. Show me what you do when the pressure comes up."

With Gary's quote in mind, this book is divided into three sections that will help you understand how to lead effectively in good times, and even more so in the bad times that inevitably surface.

Part I: The Why of Leadership

Since you're reading this book (or browsing through it in a bookstore to see if it's worth buying), you're probably wondering why leadership and leading in a certain way is important. In Chapter 1, we begin by having Todd Wolfenbarger, partner and president of The Summit Group, explain how leaders should view themselves as servants of their employees. As Vaynerchuk noted, "Humility is a huge part of leadership. Having the ambition to be all-time and equally knowing you don't mean shit is a huge, huge factor to leadership."

Chapters 2 through 5 talk about building your company culture. In Chapters 2 and 3, we explain why the leader sets the culture and how that's vital to getting an edge over your competition. Chapter 4 explains why requiring your employees to "live and breathe" company culture can backfire easily. We follow that in Chapter 5 by showing you five companies that get culture right to give you some inspiration for your own company.

We delve into the why of leading a team in Chapters 6 through 10. As a leader, one of your primary jobs is to listen to your team, and Chapter 6 explains why your team members may not be as happy as you think and what to do about it. If you're new to leadership, make sure not to skip Chapter 7, the six mistakes rookie leaders make.

Experienced or not, leader micromanagement is a killer of company culture, and Chapter 8 talks about the seven warning signs you're already the dreaded micromanager so you can correct your behavior right away. If you realize you're a micromanager but you're like so many managers and are afraid to delegate, Chapter 9 tells you why and when you should be delegating to others.

If you have a startup company, or if you run your business or team with a startup mentality, then Chapter 10 explains why radical candor—feedback that is both caring and challenging—may be the way to communicate with your team.

Finally, Chapter 11 wraps up this section and explains why you can't afford to fixate on results at any cost.

Part II: The What of Leadership

This section tells you about what you need to do to be an effective leader, and it's chock-full of tips, keys, and tools. We kick off with a reminder about the choice you need to make about running your business in Chapter 12. To be an exceptional leader, Chapter 13 lists seven traits that you need to possess to be effective. If you're not sure what you should be doing every day to be the best leader, read and bookmark Chapter 14.

Everyone has a different leadership style, and that's okay. Chapter 15 gives you five keys for being an effective leader no matter how you roll. Part of leading is requiring your team members to be accountable, and Chapter 16 has five keys for you to promote accountability.

Employee turnover is inevitable in any company, but you can boost retention by following the five touch points explained in Chapter 17. Feedback is an important part of retaining your people and helping them grow, but doing so with creative people can be challenging. Chapter 18 has good tips for providing valuable feedback for those team members. Creative people are just part of the diverse makeup of your business, and Chapter 19 gives you five tips for dealing with that diversity effectively.

It's important that you treat everyone else as a human being, and Chapter 20 has ten ways to "make nice" to employees and help them perform better. If you're thinking about other ways to boost productivity, Chapter 21 discusses three ways to decentralize management so you can decide if that's an option to explore. Chapter 22 wraps up Part II by giving you a list of tools to build and shape your culture to inspire your employees.

Part III: The How of Leadership

This section teaches you how to implement leadership and management strategies in your business, starting with the four things to do if you're a new leader. No matter if you're a new leader or a seasoned one, you need to read Chapter 24 to understand the four traits that build trust with your team. That discussion rolls right into Chapter 25, where you can learn six more strategies to build a great workplace for free from TV and radio show host Jeffrey Hayzlett.

If you want to be a better motivator, start with Chapter 26, which explains how to motivate people by putting their needs first. The diversity of the workplace means, naturally, you'll have introverts, so Chapter 27 tells you how to motivate them and help them reach their full potential. Part of that diversity in the 2020s means some people work off-site, and Chapter

28 explains the six things you must do to manage workers remotely.

This management brings its own accountability challenges; Chapters 29 tells you how to increase accountability without being a tyrant, and Chapter 30 tells you how your feedback can keep building your culture. If that culture needs fixing, read Chapter 31 to learn more about how you can fix it, as well as Chapter 32 to learn how to improve employee engagement.

We wrap up the section and the book in Chapter 33 with Bob Glazer of Acceleration Partners explaining how to lead versus manage your team's success.

As you read this book, feel free to take notes and jot down ideas. This is just the beginning of your journey toward becoming a better leader, and don't forget to share your insights with your team members—and encourage them to buy their own copy of this book!

Leadership is not about power, but empowerment. Perhaps it's best to keep the Chinese philosopher and Taoism founder Lao Tzu's words in mind: "A leader is best when people barely know he exists, when his work is done, his aim fulfilled, they will say: We did it ourselves."

PART I

THE WHY OF LEADERSHIP

PART I

THE WAY OF LEADERSHIP

CHAPTER 1

Why Leaders Should View Themselves as Servants

by Todd Wolfenbarger

Twenty years ago, I received a unique gift. This gift impacted my career by introducing me to a servant leadership model I've tried to emulate ever since.

I was living in Seattle and had taken off for Christmas Eve. It was a typical December afternoon in the Northwest—cold and rainy—and I was on my front porch with my young daughter, sprinkling homemade magical glitter oats along the path for Santa's reindeer that night. My little girl was loving the adventure, and so was I.

Amid our fun, I looked up as an unknown SUV pulled into our driveway. To my surprise and mild discomfort, my boss—our company's CEO—got out of the car. After exchanging greetings, he knelt next to my daughter and asked, "What does your daddy want for Christmas?" Taylor said, "He wants a bike." My boss smiled, opened the back of his SUV, and pulled out a mountain bike with a bow on it.

He had called my wife in the weeks before (as he had with all of his direct reports) and asked her if there was a Christmas gift—something I really wanted—that he could get for me. To say I was grateful and impressed would be an understatement.

In the years since, I've duplicated his efforts with my own team and have received similar sentiments in return. As much as my team appreciated the experience, though, I found that I loved the style of leadership even more.

The term "servant leader" was first coined by Robert Greenleaf in a 1970 essay, and it describes leaders who serve first, accepting that true leadership will be the result.

As the years have gone by, I've become convinced of this approach. I believe in the concept because I've experienced its effectiveness from both sides of the equation.

Looking to try the approach for yourself? Here are four quick ways to begin:

1. Learn Something Specific and Important about Every Person You Lead

There's a writing tip I love called "naming the dog." Calling the dog Sparky instead of just "the dog" makes a significant difference. Why? Because the specificity creates connotation, context, and nuance—all important factors in writing well.

Specificity in servant leadership is also important. Knowing personalized details of those you lead, especially those who show personal motivation, can make a big difference.

For example, I work with someone who, when told to do something in a very specific way, creates a situation that nearly forces him to go in the other direction. He's important to our team, and knowing this about his character, I try hard never to issue him any direction or feedback in a hyper-authoritative or declarative manner. To another person on my team who craves specific instruction, this approach would be frustrating. The key is to know those you lead specifically so you can serve them best.

2. Take Action Yourself, and Let the Credit Go Somewhere Else

Seth Godin's book *Poke the Box* examines the need for starters in organizations—the people who take initiative even when they don't have an edict to do so. According to Godin, initiative is the birthplace and differentiator of today's workplace leadership.

There are many reasons people fail to start something new or act now, but one of the biggest is a desire for credit (or, conversely, to avoid blame). Godin's solution? Give the credit away. Worry about taking action, and use the positive results as a gift for those you lead. It may seem counterintuitive, but this is the heart of servant leadership: as you help others succeed, you become more successful yourself.

3. Find a Millennial in Your Organization to Work Alongside

I work with a lot of people who are in the first or second jobs of their careers, and I'm learning so much from them. For example, many in this group prioritize the sharing of unique experiences over career advancement. It's a part of the ethos these younger workers exude, and I find it inspiring.

When you get interested in your employees and what matters to them specifically, you open the door to leading them. When you take the approach of a servant leader with the millennial generation, they will respond.

4. Commit and Believe

Traditionalists might argue that leadership is all about issuing orders with clarity and fairness. I don't believe that anymore. I believe it's more about showing people what they're capable of, mapping that to your company's direction, then letting them go to work.

It might seem counterintuitive because it cedes some perceived control. But in the end, it produces greater results. It's a philosophical investment, requiring a commitment and belief that the payoff will come. In my years of servant leadership, I've seen it pay off in spades.

In the end, the servant leader—the one who knows the troops on a deeper level—truly wins. As Greenleaf himself has said, "The difference manifests itself in the care taken by the servant first to make sure that other people's highest priority needs are being served." The best, and most difficult, test to administer is: Do those served grow as people?

CHAPTER 2

The Leader Sets the Culture

by Brian Patrick Eha

Y ou are leading the culture of your company workplace. The only question is: are you doing it intentionally, or are you doing it unconsciously? Let's look at four different organizations and how the leaders at each one got explicit about shaping their company culture.

Leading a Culture of Teamwork

In 2012, chef Niki Nakayama was living her dream, preparing traditional Japanese *kaiseki* feasts at her Los Angeles restaurant, n/naka. Then, her sous chef quit without notice. "I had been accustomed to splitting tasks with him," she says, but everything fell on her shoulders. She dove in, preparing exquisite, labor-intensive meals of 9 or 13 courses—but with less leadership available, her minimal staff suffered.

What was going on?

The problem may have been culture. In traditional Japanese kitchens—not unlike some traditional American offices—subordinates are expected to watch and learn, rarely ask questions, and never debate the head chef's ideas. "I am not a great teacher," Nakayama admits. That's why the loss of her sous chef was so acute: The staff had lost a certain kind of leader, someone who could "speak Niki," bringing order to her creative chaos and translating her instructions for everyone else. Nakayama couldn't fill the hole herself.

She came to a realization: Everyone should be aware of their weaknesses and overcome them as a team. Nakayama fixed her own problem by hiring Carole Iida, a fellow chef. Where Nakayama was messy and spontaneous, working off the top of her head, Iida was organized and reliable, and could guide the staff. "She brought in her organizational abilities, and we were able to put everything together for other people to understand," Nakayama says.

As a result, the 2016 Zagat guide has awarded n/naka the top spot for food among L.A. restaurants, a dramatic rise from the year before (as of 2024 n/naka has been awarded two Michelin stars). Now, Nakayama encourages all her workers to focus on their strengths—"to pull out that best part of ourselves and just contribute that all the time without spending too much time trying to fix the weaknesses that we have," she says. "It's far more productive in a team environment. It's knowing and respecting each other's strengths and weaknesses that makes a great team."

Leading a Culture of Rigor

The well-regarded nonprofit research center Santa Fe Institute (SFI) sets a high bar for scientific inquiry. More than 250 researchers affiliated with SFI are investigating the fundamentals behind the world's biggest problems, from plagues to global economics. Its president and William H. Miller Professor of Complex Systems, accomplished scientist David Krakauer, knows one thing for sure: When working with all these great minds, he cannot always be the smartest one in the room. He sometimes thinks of himself "as a colonel leading an army of generals."

So, how does he lead them? "The authority of my position is not worth shit," he says. "When I'm talking to someone who is more accomplished than I am, my opinion is not the most compelling argument. The most compelling argument is rigor. You have to speak the language of rigor."

To "speak the language of rigor" means to support every idea with observation, evidence, and analysis—and maybe even conducting experiments to determine the best course of action. It means trusting a clear, quantitative approach that everyone can understand, and it means not using language that's limiting.

Here's a phrase Krakauer hates: "That's not how we do things around here." No. He is adamant on this point: anyone caught uttering that phrase, he says, "should be put down."

Like scientists, business leaders should wield evidence as a tool of persuasion, Krakauer believes. He quotes physicist Richard Feynman, "Science is the belief in the ignorance of experts." It's a hard lesson to learn, but a necessary one: Your gut instinct is not sufficient. If you want to persuade top talent to follow your lead, you'd better be able to back up your arguments with more than your job title.

Leading a Culture of Inquiry

The tech startup Contently helps Fortune 500 companies and other brands engage in content marketing. Founded by three guys in New York in 2010, it has since grown to a staff of about 100. Along the way, cofounder and chief creative officer Shane Snow feared a disturbing change: The energy driving that growth—that scrappy, do-anything attitude—could easily diminish or even disappear. Employees might become timid in large groups, afraid of earning the ire of the majority.

"Most people and most companies reach a plateau at a certain point, and at many points," says Snow. "It's crazy how quickly even a disruptive, rebellious startup can get to the point where they say, 'That's not the way things are done here.'"

There's that phrase again.

Contently took steps to make sure that culture didn't take root. For one, Snow limits meetings that involve problem solving—that is, a situation where employees really need to speak up—to three or four people. Employees are game, Snow says: They do want to keep things fresh. A leader's role is to create the right opportunities. He challenges Contently's big team to feel scrappy by doing things like asking for ten X ideas—say, "How can we improve customer happiness by ten times?"

Time for another forbidden phrase: "Don't bring me problems; bring me solutions." Leaders use that phrase because they think it inspires employees to take initiative, says Adam Grant, a professor at the University of Pennsylvania's Wharton School and author of *Originals: How Non-Conformists Move the World* (Viking, 2016). Instead, it teaches employees not to speak up about a need unless they have a proposal for fixing it.

"When you ask for solutions, you create a culture of advocacy rather than a culture of inquiry," Grant says. "Most creativity—most innovation—happens when somebody points out a problem that's not yet been solved."

Snow wants to hear it all. He and his cofounders set aside a few free hours every week so any employee who wants to chat can do so. It's an invitation to hear about those problems that are in search of solutions. "When someone brings in a perspective that hasn't been heard yet," Grant says, "it often forces you to reconsider your decision criteria, to bring in new information—and that ultimately is good for your process."

Leading a Culture of Accountability

Bridgewater Associates is the world's largest hedge fund, managing over \$150 billion in assets for sovereign wealth funds, corporate and public pensions, foundations, and university endowments. Its founder, Ray Dalio, is widely seen as a financial genius. Yet after a meeting with a potential client one day, an employee several levels down on the org chart fired off a blistering email to Dalio. He accused the boss of being unprepared and disorganized, going so far as to give him a D-minus grade for his behavior!

"I don't know many organizations where you can send an email like that to the billionaire founder and keep your job," says Grant in *Originals*. But instead of lashing out, Grant says Dalio asked others who had participated in the meeting to assess his performance. The email exchange was then forwarded to the entire staff, effectively turning Dalio's misstep into a case study.

This is how Bridgewater's culture works, according to Grant—everyone is accountable to everyone. The staff is expected to routinely rate coworkers on a range of 77 qualities, including some—like the willingness to touch a nerve—that might not be prized at other companies. The firm's 1,500 employees can even assess their bosses; the more incisive the critique, the better. All this data, including the name of each person who left feedback, is available to any employee.

It's extreme. It wouldn't work for most companies. Thirty-five percent of new hires don't make it past 18 months. But consider what Bridgewater is going for: It wants employees to feel that hard work is recognized, and that the company values transparency. Find ways to bring those traits into your workplace—because when an employee feels comfortable enough to challenge you, and you're able to turn that into a lesson in leadership, then you've created a culture in which everyone can do their best work.

Dalio's example is perhaps the most illustrative of all the examples here. It shows just how far a CEO has to go in leading company culture. What happens at Bridgewater is what happens everywhere—culture starts at the top.

CHAPTER 3

Your Culture Is Your Edge

by Ben Judah

t is astounding that Blockbuster didn't start delivering DVDs by mail back in 1999. It would have effectively shut Netflix out of the market. When drones became popular, DHL and FedEx had the opportunity to begin exploring the option of drone delivery. They could have stayed ahead of the curve, but other companies are leading the charge there, too.

These recent innovations have shaken established industries across transportation, communications, retail, and logistics. The question is: Why is change still coming from the outside? Why do companies and even entire industries ignore innovation, and then lose market share and industry leadership to outside challenges?

It comes down to company culture.

"It's always been done this way," is one of the most dangerous phrases to be uttered in a company, and the enforcement of that thinking is the first step on the road to ruin. The thinking that exploring new methods is dangerous is flawed for one main reason: it assumes *ceteris paribus* (from Latin; loosely, "all things remaining equal"). This can only ever occur in theory—never in reality. The world is changing faster than ever before, with cultural norms evolving to catch up with the accelerated pace of technological advancement. All things are most certainly not remaining the same, and if they do, rest assured someone somewhere has a surprise in store.

The saying goes, "Failing to prepare is preparing to fail," but whose responsibility is it to prepare? Everyone's. From the CEO to the intern, the battle cry of "none of us are as innovative as all of us" lays the foundation whereby all contributions are valid *and* welcome. Each individual within a company has his or her own area of expertise, technical or otherwise, which gives insight into new ways of innovating anything from internal processes to the overarching product or service sold. Companies that are open to hearing new ideas and are agile enough to adapt to the changing tides will stay relevant for longer and maintain market share over innovative newcomers.

WalkMe—Israel's "Most Promising Startup of 2016"—has ingrained the spirit of "there is no such thing as a bad idea." As Rafi Sweary, president of WalkMe, puts it, "One of the most important ways by which we promote innovative thinking at WalkMe is that if an idea fails, there is no negativity against the person whose idea it was. If, however, an idea is adopted successfully, the attribution and appreciation for the person who came up with the idea is seen company wide. This created a culture in which everyone competes for innovation and efficiency in all things implemented at WalkMe."

This culture can only ever come from the top down: Senior company executives must empower managers to listen and encourage the sharing of ideas from their entire team. Companies can adopt this thinking as a day-to-day occurrence or one saved for special events, creating hackathons where teams work together to intensely focus on solving complex issues or creating innovative solutions to set challenges. Hackathons started as a technique often utilized for software related businesses, but now are being used as a tool to solve more issues across all different verticals.

Other companies have found ways of going one step further, in the interest of staying ahead of the curve. Google's 80/20 rule, which gave employees the opportunity to use 20 percent of their time on developing new projects, led to the creation of Gmail, Google Maps, and AdSense. Coffee behemoth Starbucks created a barista competition to keep their baristas' skills up to scratch and to strive to improve with the sense of competition.

Digital content company ironSource created an internal accelerator called ironLabs which allows the 700-plus person company to behave like a small startup. Tomer bar Zeev, CEO and cofounder of ironSource, explained how useful the accelerator has been by saying,

> *We're not only comfortable nurturing and maintaining multiple different products—that diversification is actually one of our greatest strengths. As we grew, it was imperative that we find a way to maintain that diversification, so we founded ironLabs as a space where anyone*

with an idea would have the resources to explore it. It worked perfectly, ensuring that we kept our knack for agile innovation, and even birthed a new product that is now a major business element at the company.

The platform for creating innovation will always appear in different forms depending on each individual company's needs and culture. It should be sacrosanct and seen as essential for the continued existence of a business.

How can you make sure you're not your market's Blockbuster, but its Netflix?

CHAPTER 4

Why a "Living and Breathing" Company Culture Isn't Always a Good Thing

by Jayson DeMers

I f you've been plugged into the entrepreneurial world at all in the past decade or so, you've probably heard people describe how they want all their employees to "live and breathe" the company culture. The metaphor here is designed to imply a deep commitment to that culture—usually defined as its values, character, and priorities.

Company culture is a commitment so deep that it can no longer be distinguished from employees' own individual values, character, and priorities.

It's also an interesting vision, and one that certainly has its merits. When all your employees are so deeply committed to the company, they'll be willing to work harder for their shared goals and more likely to work together. They'll also contribute more positively to the overall environment, creating an accelerated feedback loop that makes the culture even stronger.

However, a "living and breathing" company culture takes the idea of culture to an extreme that yields more than a handful of downsides, and the only reason the concept exists is because of our temporary obsession with the importance of company culture.

The Rise of Company Culture

Organizational culture has been a concept in business and management since at least the 1970s, but it's only recently that "corporate culture" has become a buzzword. You could argue that this is so because more business leaders are discovering the true objective value of a positive company culture; I'd argue, however, that it's something closer to a fad.

Company culture started to accelerate in popularity once people started realizing that many tech startups in the Silicon Valley region—which turned into multibillion-dollar juggernauts—all had surprising cultural features in common that broke from traditional office environments.

Obscure furniture, casual dress codes, and a youthful energy were, and still are, stereotypically common features in this context, and they fuel a false association. Specifically, both culture and financial success differentiate these companies, so surely, the two factors must be connected.

The end result is a still-growing obsession with creating a unique and "modern" corporate culture—one that employees must be "living and breathing" to allow for that culture's full benefits.

How Company Culture Can Go Too Far

This illustration shouldn't convince you that corporate culture is bad or unnecessary; in fact, I'd still argue that it's critical for a business' success. But we should be careful not to over-estimate culture's benefits and should avoid shoving it down workers' throats.

Company culture can go too far in at least the following ways:

- *Homogeneity.* Some of the best ideas in the world are the ones you didn't see coming. They come from outside sources and outside perspectives or arise from uncomfortable situations. Accordingly, having a diverse environment, with many different minds and perspectives, is important to the survival of a business. Being too rigid and too serious about your company culture encourages a kind of homogeneity; if all your employees think and act alike, they'll all solve problems the same way, which will limit your growth and put you at risk for bigger problems down the road.
- *Stress and pressure.* Using the phrase "living and breathing" company culture implies that working for this company is as important as life itself. While some people thrive in high-pressure environments, chronic stress isn't good for anybody. If you make your workers feel like nothing matters except their work, eventually they will begin to suffer lower morale and display lowered productivity.

- *Polarization.* Approaching company culture with this extreme level will also polarize your newest hires and job candidates. It's true that you'll naturally attract some people who already fall in line with your company values, but you'll also scare away some serious talent who may differ with you on a handful of key points. Is that scenario really worth it?

- *Misplaced values.* Don't forget that this is still a business, and your bottom line is profitability. Company culture is a useful way to make your workers happier and more productive, but the "living and breathing" angle can sometimes interfere with that vision. For example, if an employee's deviation from your cultural norms ends up earning better results for your business, you shouldn't complain or reprimand the employee.

- *Cult vibes.* Finally, to a more subjective point, enforcing your company culture too strictly or seriously gives off some serious cult vibes. This is off-putting to employees, clients, and customers alike—so try not to turn your brand into a corporate brainwashing scheme.

Finding the Right Balance

Remember that company culture is still important, and your employees should fit, to some degree, into that culture. The key is to find the balance between nurturing that culture and mandating it. It's different for every business; depending on your size, your niche, and your personal preferences, you may end up settling on one end of the spectrum or the other.

There isn't a single right answer, but you owe it to your staff and the future of your business to give it some serious analysis.

Five Companies Who Get Culture Right

by Steffen Maier

Some companies are revered for the way they keep employees engaged and passionate about their work. Here, we share with you five of the best organizations with the most engaged staff who go the extra mile, sharing the strategies and practices that keep them at the top of the employee engagement game.

1. Full Contact

Each year, this software firm offers their employees $7,500 to take a "paid" vacation. They literally pay their people to go on holiday anywhere they like. The only rules? You actually have to go somewhere and can't do any work or answer work related calls or messages. They stand by the idea that employees who actually go on vacation return to work with a different, fresh outlook. They are fully present and eager to get back to their job.

These "paid" vacations also supposedly eliminate the issue of people thinking they're the only ones who can solve a problem. Once people return from their holiday relaxed and find things running smoothly, they feel less pressure to handle everything themselves and develop a heightened sense of trust for their coworkers.

If it's not quite in your budget to give out large amounts of cash for holidays, it's always possible to let people take a couple of extra days' paid leave or a long weekend once in a while. The important thing is that they can leave their work responsibilities behind and really get away. People will appreciate their efforts being recognized and welcome the chance to disconnect from their job—even for a short time.

2. Southwest Airlines

Southwest Airlines is revered for their employee engagement practices over the years. They have a team full of committed, enthusiastic people passionate about the company's vision and values. They've set the bar high as a glowing example of customer service because of their collective of happy, committed employees.

Take something as seemingly mundane as a company uniform. The company allowed employees from any department to apply to collaborate on new designs. The results reflect the personality and company culture in a way not possible had employees not had a say. Employees were responsive to this, describing it as an "unforgettable experience."

Southwest encourages employees to do things differently, as evidenced by the viral video of one flight attendant rapping the safety information. It goes to show the kind of attitude the company has towards keeping things fun and unique by creating a great experience for customers and employees alike.

Recognizing those employees who go the extra mile is another key factor of Southwest's engagement practices. Each week, the CEO gives a "shout out," publicly praising employees who have gone above and beyond. There's also a monthly recognition in Southwest's magazine featuring an employee who shined that month. This kind of recognition keeps employees aware that they're valued and that their commitment to the company doesn't go unnoticed.

As company founder Herb Kelleher points out, competitors can't simply adopt the levels of engagement and commitment found at Southwest—it takes a special kind of employee and company culture: "They can buy all the physical things. The things you can't buy are dedication, devotion, loyalty—the feeling that you are participating in a crusade."

3. Legal Monkeys

This legal record management company established a simpler, smaller way to show employees that their hard work is valued. Their Appreciation Board is a glass picture frame where employees can write a note and present the board to someone they want to show appreciation to. Whoever receives the board is free to keep it on display on their desk until they are ready to pass it on to someone else. Each achievement also gets posted on the company Facebook page, ensuring people outside the team see the recognition.

Ideas like this are great. They're not only simple to implement without disturbing daily workflow, but they also build a real-time feedback culture, encouraging people to give positive feedback and show appreciation for their peers and coworkers.

4. Screwfix

One way this U.K.-based hardware company keeps their employee engagement levels up is by keeping an open, honest company culture. Every two weeks, employees are given the opportunity to provide feedback without rules or guidelines to their managers. They are encouraged to give feedback on everything: how things are going, how they think things are managed, how the company interacts with customers, ideas for improvement, or anything else they want to bring to their managers' attention.

A great example of how well this initiative works: employees came up with an idea for a new customer card that speeds up the in-store process by identifying customers and allowing them to make quicker purchases. Like many other initiatives now in place, this would never have come to fruition had the employees not been asked for their input.

Having this kind of regular, 360-degree feedback in place not only means things don't get overlooked as often. It also keeps the conversation going and ensures a company culture where people feel as if they make a difference—they're more than just their role and their efforts benefit the whole company.

5. DreamWorks

Although employees at DreamWorks Animation are provided with perks such as free refreshments, paid opportunity to decorate workspaces, and company parties after big projects are completed, a practice they really appreciate is that at such parties and events, they are encouraged to share their personal work and projects with their coworkers. This opens up an appreciation of non-work-related projects, boosts creativity, and makes employees feel that they are more than just the work they do for the company.

With other companies like Google also giving employees the time to work on and pitch their own projects, this is a great way to tell your employees that you not only trust them, but also that you value their input and creativity. This keeps people feeling both in control and passionate about their work.

While it may not be feasible for your company to provide huge amounts of money for "paid" holidays or assign large percentages of time to personal projects, you can take the spirit behind their practices to come up with ideas of how to implement those feelings in your own organization.

Great employee engagement is a sure-fire way to create a great company.

CHAPTER 6

Your People Aren't
as Happy as You Think

by Heather R. Huhman

When VitalSmarts surveyed 1,200 employees from various companies on workplace culture, it found that many employers were missing the mark. While leaders want to believe they've created environments filled with innovation and teamwork, there's a good chance their employees see the workplace as one of obedience, competition, and predictability. Let's contrast this ideal against what employees really think, and then look at how to close the gap.

The Ideal

As you climb the corporate ladder, the comments about a company's culture become more and more positive. These leaders dream of a workplace full of innovation; they believe they've provided the necessary tools for employees to move successfully forward. They make sure that new methods are always being created to better the work process for employees.

These visions of an ideal workplace include a culture of teamwork where employees are on the same page and working together in a productive manner. In this world, there's no such thing as generational gaps because a company's employees will all have the same training and correct amount of knowledge to complete their daily tasks.

The Reality

Unfortunately, the happiness that employers believe their employees experience isn't their employees' reality. Globoforce conducted a survey of more than 800 full-time U.S. employees and found that 47 percent of its respondents did not feel their company leaders cared about or actively tried to create a great workplace.

Maybe employers should consider a reality check: their employees are dealing with the reality of miscommunication, technology advancements and challenges, and the ever-changing nature of work. These issues, combined with the overwhelming feeling of leaders not actively trying to better the work culture, create frustration and lead to decreased productivity.

Generational gaps create tension within the ideal team-work vision. Employees from different age segments view the nature of work differently and place different values on various workplace benefits. Unify surveyed 9,000 knowledge workers and found that 16- to 24-year-olds described the ideal workplace as creative, successful, and exciting. In contrast, 35- to

44-year-olds wanted to be part of a workplace that is creative, successful, and supportive.

With one generation looking for excitement in the workplace and another seeking support, the lines get blurred with employees understanding one another when they work together. This type of miscommunication can damper employee happiness and production.

Feeling that the proper tools aren't being delivered or updated can push a company's culture into a frustrating, unproductive standstill. Companies with outdated technology, as well as those with newer technology but no ongoing training on it, are hurting themselves and their employees. Innovation and growth can't happen if employees are dealing with such hindering issues.

The Bridge

To keep current employees happy and productive, understand how employees view your culture. Give them specific goals, assure them that their frustrations are heard and addressed, and institute employee reviews.

In this context, performance-management tools like Reflektive enable real-time feedback, performance reviews, and goal alignment. Listening—and really hearing—any feedback employees have gives employers a view of reality they may not have otherwise. This new online vantage point helps employers draw a new roadmap for workplace culture.

Performance reviews in particular help employees stay connected with employers about their progress. Innovation increases when employees completely understand what needs improving. Separate reviews for each employee are important because everyone feels their performance is being reviewed from a range of job responsibilities.

Aligning goals in weekly meetings is another step. Goal setting can begin the process of closing the generational gap by encouraging teamwork. Encourage goal setting that includes all generations' point of view to bring the team closer together. For example, create guidelines that will make a task "exciting" for the younger generation and line up tools to help everyone show "support" for the older generation.

Discover what matters most to your people and deliver it.

CHAPTER 7

Six Mistakes Rookie Leaders Make

by Gordon Tredgold

The transition from technical expert to first-time leader is a difficult step and one that causes many to stumble and fail. I know this from personal experience.

In fact, I initially struggled to get the respect of my team and almost lost control and failed to deliver the project I was leading. Fortunately, I had a very supportive manager who stepped in and helped pull me through that ordeal so I could ultimately make the grade. But the lesson was clear: Too often, people are put in leadership positions without the appropriate training, and they struggle.

Here are six common mistakes that rookie managers make, which can cause them to fail.

1. *Believe they have all the answers.* When you appoint technical experts to leadership positions without the appropriate management skills, they believe that their technical experience will save them, and they

start to believe that either they have, or need to have, all the answers. This can lead team members to feel uninvolved and uncommitted. New leaders need to understand that management, like any position, brings a new set of responsibilities. It may be a humbling feeling, especially for a top achiever, to take a step back and recognize that they will now need to seek out answers in their new role.

2. *Too hands-off.* What a lot of people fail to realize is that with every promotion comes more work—not less. When leaders make that mistake, they become hands-off, sitting in their offices and leaving everything to their team. As a leader, you are heavily involved in defining the goals, setting the vision, inspiring the team, and leading the charge. Leadership is not a hands-off, paper-shuffling job; it's a hands-on job, especially when you are stepping into a new role. You need to get a feel for the job, which may mean getting your hands dirty to fully understand what the team does and what they need to accomplish the goals.

3. *Too hands on.* Just because you were the expert doesn't mean you need to be involved in everything. Your job is to lead the team—not necessarily to do the work for them. Sure, there may be times when you need to step in and get your hands dirty, but that should be the exception and not the rule. Once you familiarize yourself with the needs and responsibilities of your team, you will need to step back. This will allow your team to function with greater autonomy and come to you when there is a question or a problem.

4. *Micromanage every task.* Micromanagement is a productivity killer. No one wants their boss looking over their shoulder every two minutes asking, "Are we there yet?" It shows a lack of trust and that you don't respect their skills. It also creates great stress for the employees. You need to strike the right balance between giving them enough space to do the job themselves and checking in to see how they are doing and if they need support.

5. *Create distance.* One of the worst and most common mistakes I see with new leaders and managers is when they create a distance between themselves and the people who work for them. They adopt the "it's lonely at the top" mentality as a strategy for good leadership. Distance, however, often causes gaps in communication, which results in individuals, or teams, taking the wrong direction. When you create distance, you also make it difficult for people to feel engaged, and when teams become disengaged, results can suffer.

6. *Act like a friend instead of a manager.* It's good to be friendly, but you need to make sure that the friendship you have with your team doesn't impact your judgment or decision making. If you were previously one of the team, this can be a difficult balance to strike, as there is a good chance that you're already friends with many of them, especially if you have worked together for a while.

It doesn't mean you should immediately drop people as friends, but you need to be able to delineate between being a friend and being their boss. People will try and take advantage, but you need to be firm and do what's right and fair—and definitely don't play favorites. In the end, a good friend will respect you more for separating your friendship and your position as a manager.

It's not easy to make the transition from team member to team leader, but as you start on that journey, remember it's your job to engage, inspire, and support your team. They are the people who are going to do the bulk of the work, and your job is to put them in the position to be successful and then help them be successful.

CHAPTER 8

Seven Warning Signs You're the Dreaded Micromanager

by Aaron Haynes

Micromanagers are notorious for causing high-stress levels, low morale, loss of productivity, and dread in the office, among other negative repercussions. In fact, they are every employee's worst nightmare. A micromanaging boss kills efficiency with outdated, self-centered, and underdeveloped management methods.

But to be fair, no manager is queuing up for this undesirable role. In fact, most fear turning into a micromanager. The line between an efficient manager and a micromanager is sometimes blurred, and it's easy to cross it, unaware you're on a slippery slope to becoming a dysfunctional boss.

Let's look at the signal characteristics of a micromanager in the making:

1. *You're scared of losing control.* Because of your need to control, you're obsessed with knowing what staffers are doing, and everything must be done your way

or you're not satisfied. Therefore, you often call back work you assign because it's not up to your standards. On top of that, you dish out instructions but make it impossible for your team to input their own ideas. As a result, you stifle their creativity, communication, and self-development, while leaving no option for effective productivity. Holding on tightly to control out of fear will eventually cause you to lose it in the end.

2. *You alone have the best approach to every task.* Believing you know best, you view your employees' work as inferior. Therefore, your actions scream that their work is substandard, a strong sign that you're micromanaging. You don't give them the opportunity to use their skills, talents, and know-how. Instead, you implement all the ideas, take control of communicating with clients, and make decisions based on your knowledge. Believing you have all the answers for resolving tasks, you work on them solo. This attitude pushes employees aside, causing them to doubt their own capabilities.

3. *You're itching to lead. Leading is not a bad thing.* On the other hand, a forceful boss who is unwilling to negotiate, who is always interfering, and who is unable to offer flexibility is a poor leader. Continual interference is a sign you lack confidence in your employees. Nevertheless, there are times when it's necessary to lead, especially in large financial transactions, vital decision-making, or other important business areas requiring managerial authority. However, if you're always in the driver's seat and find it difficult to allow employees

to manage everyday tasks, this creates uncertainty and resentment. As an alternative, train staff, build trust, and support them.

4. *You suspect everybody wastes time and resources.* One of the most annoying traits of a micro-manager is their suspicion. Because you suspect everyone is either wasting time or company resources, you are always prying. You command a detailed record of phone calls, meetings, spending, tasks, or anything else you think could be wasted. This obsession puts stress on everyone. Constantly judging and prying will eventually create a lack of faith in you and drive employees out of the company.

5. *You organize endless, unnecessary meetings.* Micromanagers use any excuse to call for a meeting. Usually, these meetings have nothing to do with work productivity. They are a pretext for finding irrelevant faults. Or you attend meetings to get your points across in discussions that don't require your presence. Another sign is insisting all employees attend meetings, whether the topic is relevant to them or not. Unnecessary, drawn-out meetings end up wasting precious time, cutting into efficiency, and breeding confusion.

6. *You second-guess the practice of delegating.* Everyone has the same amount of time during the day. However, your time seems less than others. Could this be because you don't know how to delegate? Each day, you're overloaded with trivial tasks and projects that rarely get completed. Lack of delegation and

communication with your employees forces you to micromanage rather than distribute responsibilities. Instead of retracting delegated tasks, allow employees to handle jobs within their capability. Practice developing your delegation skills to reduce your workload and give employees a sense of ownership.

7. *You're trying to run a one-person show.* Perhaps you have the attitude that micromanagement means taking on everything by yourself. Consequently, you lack faith in your employees' abilities and bear the brunt of the workload. You're busy fretting about their productivity and criticizing their work, leaving you little time to manage properly. Rather than working with them to develop a competent team, you set them up to depend on you. This leads to increased workload and bigger pressures on you, amplifying the danger of impending burnout.

Finally, perhaps you have good intentions at heart, but still cross the line over into becoming a micromanager. If you identified with any of the earlier danger signs, you are now in a better position to improve your management skills. One way to improve working relationships is to get regular feedback from staff. Reflect on the response, measure yourself against their comments, and take action to implement the necessary changes. Transform yourself from being a dreaded micromanager to becoming a valued, respected leader.

CHAPTER 9

Should You Delegate That? A Comprehensive Guide

by Larry Alton

D elegating tasks is an important, yet tricky, art in the realm of entrepreneurship. It's a way to lighten your workload and distribute tasks among your employees and partners, and if you do it right, you'll end up more productive as an organization. Plus, you'll be less stressed on a personal level.

Unfortunately, though, most entrepreneurs struggle to get delegating right. They don't know when to do it or how to do it, and they end up either never delegating at all or delegating so ineffectively that they wind up with more on their plates than when they started.

So, what should you do when you're faced with the ultimate dilemma: "Should I delegate that?" Here are the steps to take to answer that question.

Recognize Your Own Biases

Your first job is to recognize any internal biases that may be affecting your decision to delegate:

- Control. Many entrepreneurs see their business as "their baby," and want to do everything they can for the business. Unfortunately, this makes many entrepreneurs reluctant—or even stubborn—when it comes to delegating their responsibilities. If this is you, you need to learn how to let go of control.

- Frugality. It's tempting, especially when yours is a bootstrapped startup, to try to minimize costs as much as possible. Accordingly, you may avoid new hires or freelancers; however, as you'll see, this too has a cost associated with it.

- Bothers. Maybe you're trying to be a kind boss and don't want to increase the workloads of others. But, remember: It's your job to assign priorities, and depending on the structure of your business, your subordinates can likely delegate further.

Determine the Value of Your Time

The key first step in deciding whether to delegate something is determining the value of your time. How much do you make per hour as a consulting rate? If you don't charge a consulting rate, how much do you imagine yourself making at a similar position somewhere else?

Once you have a rough idea of how much your time is worth at an hourly rate, you'll know the relative "value of your time," which you can use to make more effective delegating decisions.

Categorize Needed Tasks as Short-Term and Long-Term Responsibilities

Next, you'll need to determine whether the challenge you're facing consists of short-term or long-term responsibilities. For example, if your business needs a new internet provider, you probably won't want to make another switch for a long time. That makes this a short-term responsibility, so whoever you delegate this task to will only have to research companies like Verizon and AT&T once.

However, if you're trying to manage a repair at a secondary property, know that you'll likely face a similar issue in the near future, so settle on a longer-term solution, such as a new hire or a property-management service to take over. If the cost to delegate to an outside source is still less than your hourly rate, hire that source.

Determine Your Priorities

Of course, you'll also have to determine your priorities as an entrepreneur. What do you currently have on your plate? Is there a major project that only you can work on at the top of the list? If so, consider any other tasks on your agenda as secondary and worthy of being delegated. However, if all your priorities are balanced, you may not need to consider delegating at all.

Review Your Staff Availability

You'll need to think about who's available to take over your work as well. Who on your team has the bandwidth to take

49

over some of your work, and who is also making a lower relative hourly rate than you? If nobody on your team currently
meets those criteria, think about hiring a freelancer from a
service like Upwork or attempting to find a new hire on a site
like Monster to fill the void.

Create a Quick Checklist

If these considerations are too abstract for you, here's a quick
checklist to run down if you're considering delegating a task:

- Is your task list too long? Do you have too much to
  do? Check your biases and stressors here, and if the
  answer is yes, continue.
- Can this be delegated right now? If you can delegate
  a particular task to someone who knows how to do it,
  excellent. That's one less thing to worry about.
- Can this be delegated cost effectively? If you delegate
  the task to an employee, freelancer, or management
  service, will it cost less than it would if you were the
  one taking care of it? Will you pay less than your
  relative hourly rate? If so, delegating it is worthwhile.
- Will this be a problem again; and if so, is it a problem
  worth preventing? If nobody knows how to do the
  necessary tasks, and your training or hiring will cost
  more than your hourly rate, consider the future value
  that training will have.

Chances are, if you're thinking about delegating a task, it's worth finding a way to do so. You're busy and your time is valuable, so any time you can delegate work for less total cost than you'd spend doing it yourself, pull the trigger.

Finally, remember this: Much of your job as a leader isn't task-by-task execution; it's setting a course for others to do what they do best.

CHAPTER 10

Why Radical Candor Is the Feedback Method Your Startup Needs

by Emily Muhoberac

Honesty is key when it comes to feedback, but many leaders are inhibiting growth by not being honest enough with their employees.

What does true honesty look like? In 2017, a spokesperson for online clothing retailer Thread shared with BuzzFeed an example of the typical feedback an employee might receive from the CEO, which reads: "We often have moments in conversations where you quickly say your point, then stop abruptly and look at me nervously, bracing yourself and trying to perceive my reaction. It makes me feel uncomfortable. It makes you seem less confident."

This type of blunt feedback has a name: radical candor. While many entrepreneurs shudder at the thought of being so straightforward with their employees, radical candor has proved to be successful at startups like Thread.

This process works because young companies don't have the time or resources to play games when it comes to office politics or passive-aggressive approaches. And because expectations change so frequently in startups, employees need to have a clear idea of what's expected.

Honest feedback also keeps employees engaged. A 2014 survey from Officevibe shows that 98 percent of employees aren't engaged in their work when they don't receive feedback. Radical candor helps keep employees on track so companies can grow.

How Radical Candor Can Jump-Start Growth

The most valuable asset entrepreneurs have is their people, so it's important to make the most of them. At Sapper Consulting, our team consists of people with varied backgrounds and experiences, and some of our best ideas have come from our "green" employees.

Radical candor helps these young and inexperienced employees grow much faster—it allows managers to correct problematic behaviors immediately. This, in turn, allows B players to grow into A players and A players to become all-stars. Even all-stars have room for improvement, and radical candor allows every employee to reach their full potential.

Employees also trust their team members more because they know if there's something they can be doing better, someone will tell them—no more wondering where they stand or if they're being kept in the dark. Our company's employees are given the autonomy to make their own decisions because they know someone will inform them if they're not doing their jobs properly.

While radical candor helps employees grow and gain trust, it can also be used to help leaders "fire fast." When managers and employees are honest about feedback, it doesn't take long for leaders to determine good cultural fits and bad ones.

Radical candor can have a profound effect on productivity and growth, but it needs to be implemented the right way to avoid negative results:

1. Have the Right Intent

Implemented the wrong way, radical candor can quickly transform into bullying in the workplace. Radical candor is about truly investing in other employees to help them improve—not complaining about or making fun of people. After an employee receives feedback, they should feel like the other person was trying to help them improve and not trying berate them.

It's also possible to be gentle while being honest. For example, a manager could approach an employee and say, "I'd like to try to understand why you've been consistently turning work in late." The goal is to open up a dialogue to get to the root of the problem without being hurtful.

Kim Scott, the cofounder of Candor Inc., explained in a blog post for First Round Capital that Sheryl Sandberg, her boss at the time, helped spark the idea after Scott gave a presentation to the executive team at Google.

After Scott finished her presentation, Sandberg mentioned to her that she used many filler words (such as "um") while speaking. At first, Scott brushed it off, thinking it wasn't a big deal. But then Sandberg said to her, "When you say 'um' every third word, it makes you sound stupid." Scott took notice and realized she had room for improvement.

2. Make It a Habit

Giving feedback needs to become a habit. Don't wait until monthly or quarterly meetings to address issues; address them as quickly as possible.

However, it's important to always give negative feedback in private—never in front of a group. Whenever I see an opportunity for feedback, I pull that person aside and discuss it with them. This gives employees the chance to make immediate improvements rather than letting them keep repeating mistakes until they're corrected in a quarterly meeting.

In addition, employees who don't receive continuous feedback often feel nervous when it's time for reviews. When employees are used to receiving feedback on a regular basis, it feels normal and doesn't induce anxiety.

Employees who regularly receive feedback are also more likely to be engaged in their work. According to 2014 research from Officevibe, 43 percent of employees who are engaged in their work receive feedback at least once a week. That leads to happier employees and increased company growth.

3. Include Everyone

In a radical candor system, everyone's on a level playing field. The CEO should be able to receive feedback from an entry-level employee, and the executive team shouldn't be held to a different standard than everyone else. We ask all our new hires to give feedback to the CEO or executive team during their first week on the job. That way, they'll understand the culture and feel more comfortable giving and receiving feedback.

Executives also need to be open to feedback in order for the radical candor system to be effective. Career company Levo and career expert Vicki Salemi discussed this topic with Millennials to learn more about how lower-level employees interact with bosses. One accounting employee shared her story about how she discussed her working style with her manager.

She said she sat down with her manager to figure out a way the two could communicate more clearly, and he was very receptive to her ideas; he wanted to make the learning process as efficient as possible. This type of open dialogue between employees and managers not only eases workplace relationships, but it also increases efficiency.

4. Keep It Specific and Actionable

Only give feedback that is helpful and can lead to change. For example, rather than saying, "You're constantly late for meetings," say, "I've noticed you're consistently late for meetings. I've found that reviewing my schedule first thing every morning has helped me stay organized, and it may help you as well."

Positive feedback should also be specific: A simple, "Great job today" doesn't sound as sincere as, "You did a great job leading our meeting today."

All employees (even the all-stars) have room for improvement, and a combination of positive and negative feedback helps employees grow—in fact, 72 percent of employees said their performances would improve with helpful feedback from their managers, according to a 2014 survey from *Harvard Business Review.*

Growth is critical for startups, and it all begins with feedback. Radical candor is a global phenomenon in the startup world, and it can lead to a more trusting and collaborative work environment (and tremendous company growth).

CHAPTER 11

Why You Can't Afford to Fixate on Results at Any Cost

by Mike Canarelli

I f you've been in the business world for any period of time, you've likely heard someone say, "Results matter." And they do, yet focusing only on results can be a recipe for disaster.

When results are all that matter, people will do whatever it takes to achieve them. That's just one of the problems with the Results Only Work Environment, otherwise known as ROWE.

What Is ROWE?

ROWE is a management strategy that pays employees for the results they deliver rather than the hours they work. The model traces its origins to 2003, when enterprising human resources executives Jody Thompson and Cali Ressler floated the idea to the retailer Best Buy. The electronics giant became the first major corporation to implement the strategy. Clothing retailer The Gap soon followed suit. Since then, hundreds of businesses, large and small, have adapted ROWE to fit their specific industries and organizations.

ROWE, along with coworking, telecommuting, and flex time, is intended to empower workers through autonomy. The mission is to co-create a happier, hungrier, and more effective work force.

In many cases, ROWEs deliver the results intended. Employees feel a greater responsibility and no longer think of their positions as jobs. Instead, they identify with it as a career. Likewise, ROWE itself often is successful. Teams operate more efficiently and typically perform well.

What's the downside? There are issues with ROWE and very real ones.

Trust and Accountability

If you've assembled the right team, trust and accountability are a given. But complete freedom affects people differently. Getting a project done on time and under budget can be stressful, and the pressure only builds as expectations grow greater. Even good people can resort to cutting corners or dabbling in unethical behavior to continue delivering results.

Communication

In environments where collaboration or frequent communication is necessary, it may not be enough to Skype or text remotely. Sometimes, walking across the room and asking a quick question can solve an immediate pressing problem. Communication in a ROWE can be complicated and messy—especially if teams or team members are on different schedules.

Transitioning

Some employees don't do well in a ROWE. Employees transitioning from a traditional workplace may find the new rules confusing or threatening. Even for those embracing the idea, wrinkles can turn into creases with mixed messages, unclear directives, or results that are moving targets.

If the workplace allows executives to work remotely but requires customer service team members to keep standard hours, the ROWE also may need to address issues of jealousy and resentment. For a ROWE to work, everyone at every level needs to buy in. It's a major culture shift. In many cases, well-liked staff might need to be let go if they fail to keep up. This can have a deleterious effect on the team's morale.

Managing

Investing in your staff is an important building block for any business, and that means occasionally holding team-building exercises or company trips. In other words, it's more than just delegating. Managers in traditional workplace environments are part coach, part motivator, and part director. In a ROWE, managing is essentially boiled down to organizing. Unfortunately, this can prohibit growth.

Results

If results are the only focus, what happens if those results are poor? Live by results; die by results.

Best Buy's stock valuation peaked in 2006 but then tumbled steadily downward. In 2012, Best Buy hired former CEO Hubert Joly. He took a hard look at the company and its declining numbers. A year after taking the helm, Joly abandoned the ROWE strategy. The effect on the stock price was immediate. By the end of the year, Best Buy shares soared more than 28 points, from $11.67 per share on December 21, 2012, to $40.17 per share on December 27, 2013. Best Buy has enjoyed considerable success after reverting back to a standard 40-hour workweek.

Although many leaders who have switched from a traditional workplace extol the virtues of the ROWE, this type of management strategy probably works best when it's incorporated into corporate culture from the beginning. Before you embark on the road to ROWE, be sure to take a top-down look at your operation. Ask whether ROWE really is the right fit for you, your team, and your clients or customers.

The answer could surprise you.

It's also worth noting that ROWE is better suited for some industries than others. In retail sales, factories, hospitality, hospitals/medical, education, and other businesses in Ih there are specific hours to deal with customers or an ongoing need to meet customer demand as it is deemed necessary, this strategy is less likely to be effective. If tasks are location specific and visible, it is unlikely that you can use ROWE.

In other situations, in Ih teamwork is essential, there is also a less likely opportunity to enact ROWE effectively. However, knowledge-based industries in Ih work is performed "behind the scenes," such as marketing, advertising, accounting, or engineering are more likely to have success with ROWE. As with most things today, there are also the hybrids—companies that have found ROWE works in one department of the company, while not in others. For example, the advertising and marketing department may be able to work autonomously on projects, while the customer service department will need to be available as needed by customers. Many companies have tried ROWE in one or two departments to determine whether it is right for them or not.

PART II

THE WHAT OF LEADERSHIP

CHAPTER 12

Either You Run the Organization or the Organization Will Run You

by Jim Joseph

A boss several years ago gave me a very important piece of advice without even realizing it. I was asking him what hadn't worked out with my predecessor, and he responded with a one-sentence answer that has stuck with me ever since:

"He didn't run the organization; the organization ran him."

At the time, it struck me as such a simple concept, so why would anyone not get it? How could you possibly "let the organization run you?"

Boy, was I in for a surprise. The organization was in chaos at the time. There were no priorities, only deadlines. There were no plans, only panic attacks. There was no order.

That's no way to run an organization, yet everyone was running ragged.

My boss did me a huge favor in that one statement…he summed up what I needed to do in my first 30, 60, and 90 days.

I needed to prioritize the group's work, I needed to put plans in place, and I needed to establish some order to the workflows and demands of the organization. Ie my boss made that one statement to me, I didn't get caught up in the demands, deliverables, and drills that could have easily gotten me off to a bad start, just like my predecessor. If I hadn't paid attention to that piece of advice, I might have also gotten caught up in a runaway train and perhaps never gotten control of it.

It's so important to not let the demands of the day run you around, constantly forcing your priorities and putting your plans on the back burner. If you let the fire drills take control, you'll never get far enough ahead of the workload to be able to run the organization.

The organization will run you.

So, how do you avoid this common mistake?

Delegate to Others

As a business leader, it's important to not get too caught up in the work. That's what the teams are for. Let your teams manage the details and the deadlines so that you can focus more on the big picture. You can be a consultant to the team, for sure, but you don't have to do their work for them. By delegating, you can allow yourself time and space to step back and take a broader look at the organization. Now, you can work *on* the business rather than spending so much time working *in* the business. To use Ir sports analogy, you can be more effective as a manager if you are on the sidelines rather than in the middle of the action. That's why delegating work to others is so important.

Determine Firm Milestones

For key initiatives you are driving, it's important to determine firm milestones and stick to them. Don't let the demands of the day push back your timelines. Give project coordinators firm deadlines to meet and treat them like you'd treat any other business priority. If you let yourself get into "crisis mode" whenever some new business interrupts the flow of business, you will find that the organization starts moving ahead of you. It's important to remain in control, allow teams to help put out fires, and stick to the milestones you have set up.

Dedicate Time

Let's face it, the days and the weeks and the months can get away from us. Sometimes, there's no avoiding the pressures of the moment. That's why it's so important to set aside time each day to do your own work...the work you need to do to run the organization. For me, it's the early morning hours that work best to do my own work. But everyone is different, and everyone needs to find their own way. Often, managers neglect their own work while trying to manage others, and as a result, it becomes like chasing a train down the track—work doesn't stop and you can't get caught up. You need to carve out your own time. None of this is easy. As my dad says, "They wouldn't call it work if it was easy." But it's a lot harder if you have an organization that Is running you rather than the other way around. Heed the strong advice given to me back in the day, and you'll see your work produce better results.

CHAPTER 13

Seven Traits of Exceptional Leaders

by Sherrie Campbell

Emotions are the universal language. Although what triggers our emotions differs, what we feel and how we express those feelings are typically very similar. Therefore, if we can feel our own pain, then we know what it is like when someone else feels pain. Because of this projective identification, it allows us to empathize and lead others with greater awareness and increased bonding. To be an exceptional leader, we must be able to place ourselves in the shoes of another and feel what they are feeling.

1. *Self-awareness.* Great leaders are deeply knowledgeable about themselves and committed to their own personal development. To be great, we must do the same. The most influential people on earth, those who have left the most significant impact, led from the heart. Empathy is not something we learn from a book. It is gained through suffering. From our suffering, we

come to accept pain and challenge as integral parts of life and necessary for great leadership. Think about it: Would you want to follow a leader who had never suffered? How would this person know what to do or how to lead us on the front lines if they've never been there before? To be great, we must know how to lead ourselves through our own fears in order to know how to lead others through theirs.

2. *Self-control.* Empathy is most easily sacrificed when we're upset, angry, or disappointed with another person. We tend to be the most hurtful and impatient in these situations. The important thing to try and practice is taking a moment to get clear before speaking.

   Great leaders tell others when a conversation will need to wait until they are clear enough to communicate responsibly. There is wisdom to knowing that conversations can be placed on hold. We cannot be reactive and empathic in tandem. In taking some time, we are able to take in the feeling, experience, and perception of the other in a way that makes sense, or at least in a way that arouses questions that can be asked with empathy rather than accusation. We get a lot further in business when we have enough empathy for the other to make sure and harness our own self-control before we speak.

3. *Communication.* Empathy is the great healer of miscommunication. It is the emotion that moves people and situations through times of being stuck. Without empathy, solutions are forceful rather than powerful. Exceptional leaders count on empathy as a catalyst for

change. It makes communication a two-way, collaborative, reflective process. It allows for vulnerability. With empathy, people feel seen and important. To develop a working environment conducive to success, we must be able to meet people where they are. We must be able to understand, respect, and implement another person's point of view, rather than only our own. This type of communication introduces the concept of fairness into the success equation.

4. *Other-centered.* When we're empathic, we care about how other people are. Exceptional leaders ask others how they are doing, what they need, and what they feel. This increases bonding, honesty, and connection. When we have a clear idea of how others feel about what they're doing, we can better support and guide them. When others trust that we support them, they realize they're not alone and without help. We must keep in mind that if we want others to be invested in what we're doing and to respond with cooperation to what we're asking, then we must consider their ideas and how they perceive who we are. To be great, we must use empathy to guide all aspects of our lives, allowing it not only to influence what we say but also to influence how we say what we say and to direct the kinds of questions we need to ask. When these steps are taken, it naturally inspires the development of empathy within others.

5. *Boundaries.* Exceptional leaders expect to face situations where they realize the only way a person on their team can grow is to either withdraw their support

from that person or to set boundaries around their support in an effort to protect their generous nature. To remain empathic, great leaders know they must protect their hearts and put themselves first in negative situations. Through trial and error, we must also understand that there are people who can stay in our hearts but not in our lives or businesses. If we are dealing with a person incapable of empathy, we must separate from them. All it takes is one toxic person to short-circuit an entire team's path to success. It is impossible to work with someone who is constantly defensive and unwilling to listen or take feedback.

6. *Kindness.* Great leaders lead from the heart. They live the wisdom that is the kindness of their spirit; how they treat, think about, and relate to others makes all the difference when it comes to developing a cohesive team driven to succeed. When we're kind, we naturally come from a genuine and sensitive place. Exceptional leaders are kind and use empathy to guide their every word, deed, and action. When we have this, we are able to be kind—even to those we do not care for. This is not a weakness or vulnerability. To be empathic is our greatest influence over others. There is truly no human quality that will take us further in life than kindness. We must not strive just to be successful. We must strive to be exceptional—anyone can be successful.

7. *Selfless.* Great leaders give back. They understand that they get more from giving than from getting. When we give back, it increases our own quality of life and our perception of what we have, and it reminds us to

be thankful for our lives as we witness the impact we have on the lives of others. When we give back, we feel good. It reminds us of the love and abundance we have in our lives, inspiring us to continue to strive to succeed to have more and more to give back. To be exceptional, we must embrace the power that comes from giving. Giving back is relationship building. It is through involvement in our communities that we develop quality relationships, which also give back to us. People want to be linked with others who are giving. People want to work for people and companies that care. Great leaders do not want to be remembered for their net worth; they would rather be remembered for how they made other people feel.

Exceptional leaders live by the Golden Rule. To be exceptional in our own right, we must do the same. We must put ourselves in the situation of others, ask how we would like to be treated in their situation, and do our best to provide them what they deserve. The more empathy we bring to our more challenging relationship problems, business negotiations, or disciplinary situations, the more successful we will be. Empathy, humility, kindness, and understanding all come from love. There is nothing more appealing to others than to be in the presence of a loving person. Exceptional leaders live this wisdom.

CHAPTER 14

What the Best Leaders Do Every Day

by Heather R. Huhman

"Who got caught being awesome?" That's the question Alex Charfen, CEO of Austin, Texas-based training and business consultancy, asks his employees every morning at 9:17 A.M., during their daily huddle.

Charfen started this practice because he recognized that like at other rapidly growing companies, his employees weren't being properly recognized for their hard work and achievements. Rather than sit back and wait for the issue to resolve itself, he and his team made sure that every "awesome" employee felt appreciated.

"This allows everyone, from managers to first-time employees, to publicly call out individuals for exceptional service, delivery, or mentorship," Charfen told me. "Making this a daily occurrence puts our team in a service mentality, shifting their mindset to think positively about how we interact with each other, our partners, and our clients."

To shape successful workplaces, company leaders like Charfen believe their daily culture should reflect the positive efforts employees make every day. In return, those employees become engaged, motivated, and productive.

Need more ideas to perfect your company culture? Here are five other ways to become a leader employees admire:

1. Praise Often—and in Public

Most leaders understand the importance of employees, but only the best openly show their appreciation.

Employees aren't seeking handouts in expensive gifts, but rather want to know how leaders see their hard work and determination. In fact, a January 2017 survey by Officevibe found that 82 percent of participating employees said they thought of recognition/praise as better than a gift.

After hearing employees speak highly of spouses' employers who publicly praise employees, Stephen Twomey, founder of Traverse City, Michigan-based digital branding company MasterMindSEO, took the hint and applied it to his own company culture. Twomey says he finds one thing employees did exceptionally well the previous day or week and praises them in public for their work. Engaging his team with different forms of praise keeps everyone inspired and motivated. "Sometimes, it's in a group email, a shout-out on our social media, or a simple high five that everyone can see.

"Work productivity has increased by 30 percent," claims Twomey, adding, "I don't hear grumbling about being underappreciated, and no one is asking for a raise like they normally would around the beginning of the year. It turns out, people really want to be inspired and led—not managed."

2. Send Employees Out with a Road Map

Effective communication and motivation go hand in hand. Employees who are unsure about their daily tasks rarely get the opportunity to go above and beyond. If their everyday tasks are unclear, how can they focus on improving them?

Ensuring employees are on the same page and know they're part of a team boosts company morale and productivity. That's why Jordan Scheltgen, cofounder and managing partner of content marketing company Cave Social, in Los Angeles, opens every day with a new process to help employees focus and achieve their goals.

"We started a program we call Attack the Day," he explained to me. "This is both a mindset and process. It starts with a 20-minute meeting every morning. Teams break off and list what they want to get accomplished for the day. Then, team members are encouraged to jump in and offer assistance to other staff members on tasks they can provide value on."

3. Capture Feedback—and Actually Use It

Keeping track of employees' feelings—especially when one of them is frustrated—is a difficult task. This is an even bigger challenge to tackle as businesses and technology expand. However, without attempting to understand your employees' feedback, your ability to retain employees and improve your company processes may become nearly impossible.

During a time of rapid growth at his own business, Benjamin Snyers, managing director and partner at New York City-based social agency Social Lab, knew he needed to keep a close eye on his team members' weekly pulse. Using Butterfly, a personal management coach, Snyers said he discovered his team was feeling stressed and overworked. As a result, he formally communicated his gratitude to his team members for their hard work, recognized their sacrifices, and explained why their efforts were not in vain.

After hearing feedback from employees and actively listening, Snyers said he understood his team's frustrations and was able to show them that the company leadership was 100 percent behind them.

4. Cultivate a Positive Workplace Culture

Motivating employees to reach the height of their potential is every leader's job. Addressing motivational issues only once every quarter—or worse, once a year—drains employees' productivity and passion for their role.

At advertising and marketing agency Gavin Advertising in York, Pennsylvania, CEO Mandy Arnold empowers and engages employees every day by creating a positive workplace culture. "We incorporated 'We Culture' team shout-outs," she told me. "Every Monday, we take five minutes for teammates to thank someone—out loud—for doing a great job. It could be a nod to the effort behind a great media placement secured or an SEO specialist who went above and beyond to solve a client issue on a tight timeline."

Frequent positive reinforcement, like the kind Arnold implements in her culture, brings out the best in employees. So, ensure the best talent stays and grows at your company by proving to your employees that their company leaders are invested in bringing the team together and helping them reach their greatest potential.

5. Ask for Feedback—and Prepare to Be Surprised

Miscommunication doesn't happen solely when employees don't understand a leader's expectations. It also happens, and leaves a lasting negative impact, when leaders aren't fully aware of employees' needs.

After feeling he wasn't performing at his best, motivational speaker Sean Douglas of Goldsboro, North Carolina, realized he was giving employees feedback but wasn't asking for it in return.

"I decided to ask for their feedback, and I was very surprised by their response," Douglas said. "I thought I was awesome but was actually lacking in some areas. Now, I am personable with them. I ask for their needs, and I also ask for feedback on how I'm doing as a leader and mentor."

Understanding what his team needs gives him the ability to lead according to their strengths, Douglas said. When leaders push their own opinions and agendas aside, they make room for their team to reach their full potential.

CHAPTER 15

Five Keys to Inspiring Leadership, No Matter Your Style

by Gwen Moran

Forget the stereotypical leadership image of a buttoned-up person in a gray suit hauling around a hefty briefcase. Today, standout leaders come in all shapes and sizes. They could be a blue jeans-clad marketing student running a major ecommerce company out of their dorm room. Or they might be the next salt-and-pepper-haired, barefoot Steve Jobs, presenting a groundbreaking new device at a major industry conference.

"Our research indicates that what really matters is that leaders are able to create enthusiasm, empower their people, instill confidence, and be inspiring to the people around them," says Peter Handal, chairman and CEO of New York City-based Dale Carnegie Training, a leadership-training company.

That's a tall order. However, as different as leaders are today, there are some things great leaders do every day. Here, Handal shares his five keys for effective leadership.

1. *Face challenges.* Great leaders are brave enough to face challenging situations and deal with them honestly. Whether it's steering through a business downturn or getting struggling employees back on track, effective leaders meet these challenges openly. Regular communication with your staff, informing them of both good news and how the company is reacting to challenges will go a long way toward making employees feel like you trust them and that they're unlikely to be hit with unpleasant surprises.

   "The gossip at the coffee machine is usually ten times worse than reality," says Handal. "Employees need to see their leaders out there confronting that reality head-on."

2. *Win trust.* "Employees are more loyal and enthusiastic when they work in an environment run by people they trust. Building that trust can be done in many ways. The first is to show employees that you care about them," explains Handal, suggesting that you take an interest in your employees beyond the workplace. Don't pry, he advises, but ask about an employee's child's baseball game or college graduation. Let your employees know that you're interested in their success and discuss their career paths with them regularly.

   "When employees, vendors, or others make mistakes, don't reprimand or correct them in anger. Instead, calmly explain the situation and why their behavior or actions weren't correct, as well as what you expect in the future. When people know that you aren't going to berate them and that you have their best interests at heart, they're going to trust you," says Handal.

3. *Be authentic.* "If you're not a suit, don't try to be one. Employees and others dealing with your company will be able to tell if you're pretending to be someone you're not," explains Handal. That could make them question what else about you might be inauthentic. Have a passion for funky shoes? Wear them. Are you an enthusiastic and hilarious presenter? Get them laughing. "Use your strengths and personality traits to develop your personal leadership style."

4. *Earn respect.* When you conduct yourself in an ethical way and model the traits you want to see in others, you earn the respect of those around you. Leaders who are perceived as not "walking their talk" typically don't get very far, notes Handal. This contributes to employees and other stakeholders having pride in the company, Ih is an essential part of engagement, adds Handal. Also, customers are less likely to do business with a company if they don't respect its values or leadership.

5. *Stay curious.* "Good leaders remain intellectually curious and Id to learning. They're inquisitive and Is looking for new ideas, insights, and information," Handal says, "The best leaders understand that innovation and new approaches can come from many places and are Is on the lookout for knowledge or people who might inform them and give them an advantage."

"The most successful leaders I know are truly very curious people. They're interested in the things

around them, and that contributes to their vision," says
Handal.

It's worth noting that Handal's recommendations do not
require training or even years of Ie. Each of the keys mentioned comes from within the individual leader. To be the best
leader you can be and bring out the best in others stems solely
from an internal desire to have the resolve to face challenges or
to be authentic, or the desire to stay curious and keep learning.

CHAPTER 16

What it Means to Promote Accountability in Your Business

by Martin Zwilling

t's easy to emphasize accountability with your team, but not so easy to tell them how to be accountable. It's even harder to make them want to be accountable—especially since many business leaders forget they are the role models for accountability. And, in fact, they don't audit their own actions to make sure they always practice what they preach.

It's also imperative that accountability become more than a buzzword, which is continuously bantered about. It needs to be a cornerstone of the employer-employee relationship. Like most aspects of business, accountability must start at the top with leaders and managers saying what they will do and doing what they have said.

I recently read Subir Chowdhury's *The Difference: When Good Enough Isn't Enough*, which shines a light on both of these issues. Chowdhury is one of the world's leading management consultants, and he argues that accountability is only one part of a caring culture that must be built and maintained to achieve sustainable, competitive improvement.

The other key parts of a caring culture include nurturing employees and leaders who are straightforward, thoughtful, and resolute in their approach to the business. All my years of experience in business resonate with that assessment and allow entrepreneurs to explain to team members what accountability means and what steps are required to get there:

1. *Be willing to proclaim that something needs to be done.* We all know of examples where employees and managers see the same problem occur over and over again but never raise a flag about it. Being accountable for doing something, or for changing something, needs to start by addressing what needs to be done or changed and making a conscientious effort to take the lead on an action step.

2. *Accept personal responsibility for tackling an issue.* Apathetic people are quick to point the finger at someone else or defer by saying "It's not my job." Leaders must send the message—and show by example—that finding quality solutions to meet the needs of customers is everyone's job, no matter how large the business. People must understand that customers are at the root of the company's success, and those working on problems must be rewarded.

3. *Make positive choices or decisions to act.* Employees who don't think they have enough training or sense of the mission will shy away from making big decisions,

which is vital for accountability. Make sure your company empowers its employees through positivity and a sense of trust.

4. *Think deeply about the consequences of each choice.* Are you working to get a problem off your back, or are you only serving your ego? Are you creating the best long-term solution for the customer, or are you merely using an expedient solution? Think before you act.

5. *Set high expectations for yourself and your team.* When you set your own sights high, you cannot help but inspire others. When you know others are taking their lead from you, it's easier to stay accountable. Inspired team members will then set their own targets higher, and that momentum will lead to better customer experiences and business success.

To make a real difference in your business, you need to be the role model for accountability. This begins by nurturing a caring mindset across the entire organization. Here are three things you need to look for in order to develop and exhibit a caring mindset:

1. *Direct and open communication.* Managers need to be transparent with their team and encourage the team to be straightforward with them and with each other. Communication suffers when people don't trust that they will be treated fairly. Too often, leaders hide business realities and personal mistakes, but expect everyone else to understand and do the right thing. Remember, everything starts at the top, including openness, communication, and trust.

2. *Individual empathy and thoughtful listening.* Real listening involves not just hearing what others say, but trying to put yourself in their shoes and fully understand the message. For managers, this requires getting out from behind their desks, visiting factory floors, meeting with employees, and being accessible at any time to their team.

3. *Passion and perseverance.* Every problem can be resolved with a mindset of passion, determination, and perseverance, and every situation can be improved. It requires humility and a willingness to change and adapt—even an acceptance that continuous improvement is the norm—but it's worth it. Passionate people don't ever settle for less than their personal best.

Accountability isn't easy. It can't be accomplished by edict, but it can be taught through example by leaders who practice the principles they want their team to follow—leaders who build a mindset of caring throughout the organization. How long has it been since you took a look in the mirror at yourself and asked if you've held yourself accountable and done what you set out (and told others) that you would do?

CHAPTER 17

Boost Retention through Training

by Sam Bahreini

etention is crucial to the success of any company. Unfortunately, it's difficult for retail employers to reduce their turnover. The best way to improve retention rates is investing in employees and their professional development.

Learnkit's 2015 report titled "Creating a Win-Win-Win Learning Strategy for Your Organization" found that 89 percent of the 421 employees surveyed feel it's important their employers support their learning and development. With most employees craving growth, why aren't companies stepping up their development game?

Let's take a look at how retail employers can improve their retention by focusing on training their employees throughout the employee lifecycle.

Hiring

It all starts here—finding top talent and sending out offers. It's best to base hiring entry-level employees on their attitude and on the degree to Ih they share company values. This way, employers know new hires are engaged in their work for more than just a paycheck. It's then up to employers to educate their candidates on what the company stands for.

First of all, promote core values to candidates on the careers page and relevant social media accounts. Then, start sharing employee testimonials that describe how current staff members put these values into action.

The main challenge is translating abstract terms and phrases into action, and that's why it's crucial to get job descriptions just right. Integrate core values into the postings and show what kinds of behaviors reflect them.

For example, if the company values growth and innovation, describe a behavior that would reflect that, like an employee who actively seeks learning opportunities and jumps in when new responsibilities present themselves. To screen for this, ask behavior-based interview questions so candidates share past Ies to prove they act according to their employer's values.

Training

This is arguably one of the most common pain points for retail companies. A 2015 infographic from the "State of Employee Training" survey conducted by West Unified Communication Services found that one-third of the 200 full-time employees surveyed said current training programs aren't productive, while Ir one-third replied that the material is not interesting or engaging.

The simple fact Is that one-size-fits-all onboarding sets new hires up for failure. They want more than boring slide-shows and packets of paper.

Break up training into modules that cater to the role and emphasize the big picture. For example, when training sales reps, give them some context on why the company values honesty and how customer satisfaction retains customers and improves sales. Make the training interesting and engaging by using games, integrating educational programs and applications, and role playing.

Coaching

Training should get new hires off their feet and onto the floor. It's on the frontlines that they learn the most Ie supervisors and management can focus on coaching them in real time. This is where creative role playing comes in.

With creative role playing, employers can coach new hires on how to interact and react in hypothetical situations. They should enlist the help of current employees to present common scenarios. Not only does this help new hires learn, but it also acts as a great tool for team building.

Role playing creates a safe place to show new hires how to deal with conflict resolution and improve their communication skills. Start introducing them to common situations where they need to apply those specific actions and behaviors they learned from the training guidelines and observe to see how they perform.

Mentoring

After onboarding, connect new hires with more Ied employees. Mentors help them build communication and customer service skills in real time. They can also empower new hires with constructive feedback and recognize them when they succeed.

New technologies Ie introducing video into the mix to help managers capture and assess performance. These video solutions are perfect for companies that want to establish an employee recognition program where they can review how employees perform and then offer an incentive or reward for the A players.

Employee recognition helps engage employees and keep them motivated. Make sure to celebrate each employee equally with a focus on new hires.

Succeeding

Create a succession structure with assistant managers and department supervisors to ensure that when a manager leaves, there is a smooth transition. Don't get caught off-guard and have to scramble for replacements.

With a strong training program, companies are more equipped to boost retention and build a talent pipeline. This way, when higher-ups vacate, there are plenty of qualified employees ready to jump in and take over.

Integrating technology into employee sourcing and talent management is the best way for organizations to stay relevant and to prepare for the future of the retail industry. When companies invest in their staff's professional development, employees want to stay and grow.

CHAPTER 18

Five Tips for Giving Feedback to Creative People

by Will Meier

I t doesn't matter if you hire the most talented, creative minds in the world—internal or external—at some point, you'll have to give them feedback. And that's where things can get dicey. Giving great feedback is an art in itself. But giving great feedback on creative work is really hard to do. You have to be specific without being overbearing. You have to guide the project without manhandling it. Make no mistake: Bad feedback can poison a project faster than almost anything else. The feedback you give—and the way you give it—can be the difference between a project everyone loves and a project everyone wishes had never started in the first place.

Don't panic. Here are five ways to improve the way you give good feedback.

1. Always Go Back to the Goal

One of the hardest parts of giving feedback is figuring out where to start. Most feedback is a mixture of emotions, personal taste, and critical thinking. This makes it just as difficult for the person receiving the feedback as it is for the person giving it.

Luckily, designers Adam Connor and Aaron Irizarry laid out a very helpful framework for thinking through feedback in their book *Discussing Design*. Forcing yourself to answer these four questions is a great starting point for getting your head around what's wrong—and what's right—with a design (or a film or a tagline or anything, really).

- *Question 1:* What is the objective of the design?
- *Question 2:* What elements of the design are related to the objective?
- *Question 3:* Are those elements effective in achieving the objective?
- *Question 4:* Why or why not?

Using this framework will help you take yourself, your emotions, and your biases out of the equation so you can focus on giving feedback that is objective, goal-oriented, and—most importantly—useful. As a bonus, these questions are also a great way of making sure you understand the goals of the project. If you have a hard time answering Question 1, then there's a good chance the project is about to come off the rails.

2. Don't Count On "Knowing It When You See It"

"I'll know it when I see it," is code for, "I have no idea what I want." This often leads to a situation where a creative is just guessing at what will make a client happy, rather than thinking critically about the ultimate goals of the project. It's a terrible place to be as a creative—especially for a freelancer on the outside of an organization—and it's a terrible place to be as a client. The remedy to this problem is twofold: 1) Go into the project with a very clear picture of what you want and why you want it. Find inspiration online that you can share. Understand what you like about the example and why. Then, 2) realize that the final product will never be exactly what you had in mind. Often, it will actually be better if you're willing to see it.

3. Be Specific

Intuition doesn't come with a vocabulary. Where a lot of feedback goes wrong is in the misinterpretation of jargon. What does "fresh" mean? What makes something "visceral"? Often, it can seem like you and your creative colleague are on the same page, only to find out in the next round of revisions that you're on completely different planets. But even without the proper vernacular, you can find ways of getting specific about what it is you're feeling/seeing/wanting. Include examples of what you're talking about. If you want something to feel fresh, include a design that feels fresh to you, or be specific about what in the design doesn't feel fresh. If you want snarky copy, show 'em some snark. Make sure you share sources of inspiration, your influences, and the things you like. Remove the guesswork, and don't let jargon get in the way of clarifying what you want. Include Google image links.

4. Take Time to Give Good Notes

Creatives put a lot of time and more than a little heart into the work they deliver to you. So, it can be very discouraging for them to receive feedback that feels dashed off, untimely, and thoughtless—even if that feedback is, in itself, very good. In the now classic book, *Creativity, Inc.*, Pixar cofounder and president Ed Catmull reveals Pixar's standard for a "good note." Our team at Musicbed has found this is a great litmus test for any piece of feedback you give. Here's Ed:

"A good note says what is wrong, what is missing, what isn't clear, what makes no sense. A good note is offered at a timely moment, not too late to fix the problem. A good note doesn't make demands; it doesn't even have to include a proposed fix…. Most of all, though, a good note is specific. 'I'm writhing with boredom,' is not a good note."

Don't rush your notes. Don't dash something off. You don't have to have the solution (in fact, it's often better if you leave that to the creative). Just start a productive conversation. The time you take to make sure your feedback meets the requirements above will be rewarded.

5. Be Quick to Praise

A little bit of praise goes a long way. Creatives will always do better work for people and projects they care about. So, be sure to communicate what you like about a piece, what you appreciate about what they are bringing to the project. Hearing what's working can be as informative as hearing what isn't. Give them something to hang their hat on, something that makes them take pride and ownership in the project, rather than begrudgingly trudging through your long list of changes. Empower your creative colleagues to bring their talent to the table. Isn't that why you hired them in the first place?

It should not take great effort to force yourself through the arduous process of giving good feedback. It takes a positive approach. Nonetheless, many people are jaded. But trust me, giving good feedback is worth it. Not only because you'll get a better product in the end, but because working through the process of giving good feedback will sharpen your skills as a marketer, a communicator, a business owner—a person, basically. Before you shoot off confusing, discouraging feedback, remind yourself why you care about the project in the first place. Remind yourself what your colleague brings to the table. Stay positive and your enthusiasm will transfer to your team. And believe me, you're all going to need it by round 11.

CHAPTER 19

Deal Better with Workplace Diversity

by Chidike Samuelson

D iversity is a good thing. Always has been. Always will be. But, still, it can be just as dangerous as it is good. While a diverse staff can be a great thing and bring amazing new perspectives to the table, it can also cause palpable tensions that destroy whatever benefits have already been brought to the table.

The reason is obvious: People are touchy about issues like race, religion, politics, and personal orientation; yet understanding "diversity" can help you become a better manager and employer. Here are a few tips.

1. Recognize the Many Types of Diversity

As already stated, diversity has many categories, and not all are readily noticeable. To notice them, you have to peer a little deeper. One key reason many people feel comfortable in one workplace, but unfulfilled in another, may be because they are diverse in those subtle little ways.

That all your staff hail from the same state doesn't mean they are not diverse. For instance, you will be aware of the obvious diversities, such as race, religion, and gender, but you also need to find out about the guy who always slinks away from birthday celebrations; you need to notice the diversity of thought among your staff members.

The meaning of diversity has changed. Factors can be as simple as height or age. People may, rightfully or wrongfully, feel that they are singled out, or treated differently, because they are shorter or taller—21 or 61. As an astute manager, you need to pay attention to how people feel they are being treated, especially if an uncomfortable situation arises. Be careful, however, not to jump the gun and assume how someone will react.

2. Redefine Discrimination, and Clamp Down on All Its Forms

In a friend's company, where most of the staff worked remotely and hailed from diverse nations, "Hello Jimmy, how is Africa?" addressed to a man named Jimmy, who actually was working remotely from Africa, degenerated to a racist slur when voiced repeatedly.

Discrimination is the most common result when people are uncomfortable with diversity and the reason that workplace diversity can be harmful at times. The Workforce Diversity Network has redefined discrimination to include actions both intentional and unintentional, conscious and unconscious—all of which should be recognized and acted on by the manager closest in contact with the offending staffer.

3. Celebrate Diversity in All Ways Possible

Nikos Antoniades, CEO of easyMarkets, was asked in a 2016 interview, shortly after he took that job, how he handled diversity.

"Our clients are based in over 160 countries around the world," Antoniades replied. "I love the unique perspectives brought to the table, and I particularly enjoy the many celebrations we have—including the Chinese Moon Festival, Polish National [Independence] Day, and our Brits this year [who] celebrated Pancake Day. Recently, we celebrated Carnival, which kicked off with a barbeque at work and was followed by a week of dressing up in costumes. Most of the celebrations are around food—who can complain?"

Moving out of your comfort zone to other people's once in a while is a sure-fire way of maintaining Ium in a diverse workplace.

4. Keep Reaching Out

Keep trying to learn about your staff, especially the new hires. Talk to them personally and find out where they are from.

Vincent Seglior, who was the World Trade Institute's director of international training for 12 years, advises in a 2012 blog post that managers should place new hires who are from a different culture under longer-term staff who are from similar backgrounds, but have become more integrated.

It's necessary to maintain the company culture, but to do this, you may have to hold an orientation session any time there are personnel changes in your department. Be a manager who develops open relationships with your diverse staff. Talk to them positively—both in a group and individually.

According to Seglior, if you remain curious about, receptive to, and open to learning about people's different cultures, your staff will benefit, and so will you. But remember, there is a difference between curiosity and prying. People from all over the world want to be respected and as such not singled out as "the guy from Nigeria" or "the woman from Belgium."

5. Don't Assume People Understand Your Jokes

Workplace jokes are often what make work fun, and the resulting camaraderie is what makes people look forward to coming to work the next day or to the next online meeting. Yet certain jokes and comments must be carefully censored.

A former manager I know made a joke in a staff meeting about people who didn't go through college. I understood that he was trying to be funny, and it really would have been funny had there not been a fair number of people among the staff who hadn't gone through college. I saw their faces turn red, literally, and the manager didn't even notice.

Not everyone has your Ie or privileges. You need to know your staff well and be sensitive to their differences. Don't assume they ought to get your joke Ie the next time you pass them over for a promotion, they may think it's Ie of their differences.

That being said, a diverse work force creates differences and some challenges, but if handled well, it can explode with benefits.

CHAPTER 20

Ten Ways Bosses Who "Make Nice" Bring Out the Best in Their Employees

by Sherry Gray

Leaders do not have to be mean to be effective. Authoritarians tend to think that by being soft they will reduce their staff's respect and motivation. Steve Jobs, for example, was famous for being mean, critical, and tyrannical to his employees.

But successful leaders are rarely like Steve Jobs. He's the exception that proves the rule. Studies show that overly rough bosses spawn motivational problems with their staff. The stress of working under a mean boss can negatively affect employee health.

A 2015 study at the University of London discovered a significant link between cardiovascular disease and management-induced stress. Researchers at the University of Concordia found that when employees think of themselves as highly stressed, their health insurance costs skyrocket by nearly 50 percent. The Institute of Naval Medicine found that a hard-core management style drives away the best talent, leaving behind only those who perform at a lower level. And conclusively, Esprit de Corps ran a poll that indicated most employees would rather have a nicer boss than receive a substantial pay raise.

The bottom line: People leave bad bosses—not bad jobs.

A considerate boss boosts cohesiveness and productivity, and leaders perceived as compassionate motivate their subordinates to be more helpful to colleagues and more Id to their teams.

Here are ten ways in Ih the boss "making nice" pays off:

1. *Let them know where you stand.* Mastering the art of kindness takes commitment and determination. But it's worth it. Real kindness is shown in straightforward and direct interaction with employees, so they know where they stand and why. You don't have to pull your punches to be kind. When someone knows you're genuinely concerned about them, they are willing to listen to your input—both positive and negative.

   Outplacement data compiled in 2016 by Mullin International over the previous three years shows 60 percent of departing employees will remain in their former company's eco-system as buyers, suppliers, influencers, or competitors. Treating your employees well pays off in multiple ways even if they aren't with you anymore.

2. *Strong doesn't have to be harsh.* Leadership means strength, but not harshness. A soft answer turns away wrath and keeps employees better balanced. When your staff sees that you can maintain poise and self-control, even under the most difficult and

demanding situations, they are more willing to follow your lead and make their own sacrifices for the good of the team or department or company. A smart boss does not jump in to take control at the first sign of trouble. They guide workers to work out their challenges In a way that Is not confrontational.

3. *Confidence is not arrogance.* Confidence, like measles, is contagious. Employees want to be around a confident boss, but shun the company of a know-it-all. The best way to show confidence is to show competence that you really know what you're talking about. And then, if you really don't know something, confess it and find the employee/team member who does know about it and learn from them.

   Great leaders are humble. They don't put up artificial barriers between themselves and their employees. Their door is Is open, and they don't require others to do things they can't or won't do themselves.

4. *Be positive, not delusional.* To remain positive yet keep your feet on the ground and your head out of the clouds is a remarkable skill that not every manager or supervisor can master. It takes some trust in others to follow through and enough confidence in your own abilities to remain unperturbed when the you-know-what hits the fan. And it will. It Is does. So, don't just say the glass is half full; instead, get your employees to see that the glass needs a lot more than only they can provide.

5. *Teach—don't preach.* The corporate world is full of people who believe they should do unto others before others do it unto them. A great boss is one that makes

the time to instruct employees in their duties and responsibilities, but is not stingy with praise. Chewing out an employee for anything, whether it's a bad habit or careless work, leaves a bad taste in everybody's mouth.

6. *Grin and bear it.* Your team will back you up just as far as they feel that you will back them up. So, go for broke. Show them that you'll "take a bullet" for them. It's not an easy thing to do, but if you're prepared to do it when the occasion arises, you can be sure they will have your back from then on—and that's a wonderful feeling for any boss to have.

7. *Strive for balance.* Employment isn't a birthday party, where everybody gets cake and ice cream and plays games all day. But neither should it be slavery in a salt mine, with the whip Is cracking. There's a balance—a delicate one that bosses have to maintain between a fun work environment and a productive work environment. Sometimes, it has to be fine-tuned down to each individual. But your people should Is be aware that you're striving to make things pleasant for them, while still expecting them to meet their goals.

8. *Be personal but not intimate.* Find out about your staff's family and hobbies and ambitions outside the office. Remember birthdays and anniversaries. Show concern when there's a health crisis with an employee or someone close to them. Let them talk about their pets. But when the talk turns to romance or finance, that's when the wise and kind boss quickly finds somewhere else to be. Show you care, but stay out of the drama.

9. *Provide fearless feedback.* Feedback can be either positive or negative. Find opportunities to discover your workers doing something right and praise them for it. When you have to deliver negative feedback, Is end the conversation by sincerely asking, "What can I do to help?" A boss is not doing an employee any favors by procrastinating when it comes to giving negative feedback. Get it over with and ask the golden question. The solution can start that much sooner.

10. *Sharing is caring.* A great boss will share credit. Ladle out sincere praise like gravy. Sincerely enjoy the success of their subordinates. Kindness is never about you—it's Is about the other person. Live for others, and your own life, at work and at home, will prosper.

CHAPTER 21

Three Ways to Decentralize Management and Boost Productivity

by Dusty Wunderlich

C orporate structures are flattening. One big reason why is that the strict hierarchies of yesteryear are no longer effective for today's fast-paced, tech-driven industries. It is no surprise, then, that major companies are shaking up their management styles.

Take the example of Zappos. The shoe company famously runs as a holacracy in Ih employees self-organize instead of operating within a traditional bureaucratic structure. And consider that after CEO Richard Lepeu retired from his position at the Swiss luxury brand Richemont, the company eliminated the position altogether. Instead, the 20 "maisons" (the brands under Richemont) now report directly to the board of directors, distributing responsibility more evenly throughout that expansive organization.

Startups should take notice of this trend and embrace it. After all, new companies usually operate with constrained resources, Is seeking ways to stretch their capital. And specialization is neither cost-effective nor likely to lead to the best early-stage products. Decentralization, however, encourages collaboration, efficiency, and speed.

Specialization is the Death of Early-Stage Innovation

Interdisciplinary integration enables startups to launch and grow quickly. Too often, entrepreneurs fail to build the right teams, Ih is one of the top reasons startups fail. Businesses falter, meanwhile, if they lack versatile employees willing and able to jump in wherever they see a need.

Highly specialized startups also do not go to market quickly. When only a handful of people in a company are qualified to work on product development, the business can launch just one project at a time. However, companies that hire multi-talented employees develop MVPs faster, get to market sooner, and iterate on customer feedback before siloed startups have even held their first launch.

Strategic hiring, then, can ensure that a startup will use 100 percent of its resources all the time. My company got in on this trend early: Rather than hiring a PR pro who deals strictly with media relations, we recruited a communications specialist who fit a variety of roles. A good rule of thumb for startups is that everyone should be able to do everything.

Ranch-Style Leadership

At our company, our culture has deep ties to our rural ranching roots in northern Nevada. That fact reflects on our work style as well. Ranchers after all are a self-sustaining bunch who use collective ingenuity to achieve their goals. Any one of them could change a truck tire or set a horse's broken leg.

This is the kind of interdisciplinary skill set we want our team members to embody, too.

In fact, this "ranch mentality" has driven our exponential growth Ie every one of our employees is comfortable taking initiative and working wherever needed. Most important, our employees understand their roles within the broader organization and how their work impacts our customers.

Don't get me wrong—even we have a loose hierarchy to ensure accountability for both ourselves and our clients. The key is breaking down the walls that keep departments and individuals from working together. When employees work in silos, they become disconnected from the customer Ie, unless they're working on a customer service team. Software engineers, for example, will build the user interface for their companies' websites, but rarely do they understand how user Interface Impacts customer acquisition.

By facilitating collaboration between departments, such as engineering and marketing, employees understand how their work assignments fit together in service of their audiences. Startup leaders can use the following strategies to create decentralized businesses:

1. Rethink Structure

Forget about traditional hierarchies, especially in the early days. There may come a time when a more traditional approach works for an organization, but the startup stage is not it. Hierarchy-induced stress has long been linked to heart disease, among other health issues, and it increases voluntary turnover by 50 percent.

So, avoid these stress-related pitfalls; organize employees into autonomous squads that can work across disciplines.

Foster a sense of equality by encouraging conversations among staff members of all Ie levels. My company practices department shadowing, in Ih founders and executives learn what people are doing throughout the organization.

When the concierge receives visits from the COO, and the vice president of marketing sits in with accounting, employees understand that we're all part of the same team, pursuing shared objectives.

2. Create a Team of "Intrapreneeurs"

Startup employees make the best intrapreneurs Ie they're involved in so many areas of the business, they have unique views on what types of products will resonate with their markets. Google's intrapreneurship program, for example, empowers team members to pursue their ideas without Ig approval from their bosses. They can partner with colleagues to explore concepts and potentially create new products for the company.

Cultivate a similar mentality by inviting employees to build new solutions and collaborate with their co-workers on ideas. Trust them to take initiative; don't require them to get a manager's green light before acting. Not only will this spur innovation, even as the company leaves the startup stage, but it will also inspire employee loyalty and enthusiasm.

3. Rally around a Common Goal

Shared goals are a great way to bring people together and drive results. And while 75 percent of employers in one 2012 to 2013 survey by Queens University in Charlotte, North Carolina, rated collaboration as "very important," 39 percent of employees reported that their organizations didn't collaborate enough.

My own company decided to emphasize sales volume one year, and every department worked toward specific origination goals. Not only did each team's members want to perform the best, but they didn't want to let one Ir down. No one wanted to be the reason we fell short, so everyone worked harder to ensure we hit the target.

We also created opportunities for cross-collaboration, so different departments could gain insights into one Ir's processes as we pursued the goal. People work together best when they understand what's happening within each department and empathize with the unique constraints and pressures their colleagues Ie.

A shared goal helped us foster more empathy and camaraderie between and among groups. We enjoyed our best sales year ever and saw an increase in proactive behavior throughout the company.

In sum, the flattened structure approach enables startups to run on all cylinders at all times. Employees can burn out when working in silos Ie they feel that the success of a particular project falls on them alone. Alternately, flat teams share responsibilities and energize one Ir through collaboration. The personal, innovative nature of holacratic startups makes them more agile and better equipped to take on their markets.

CHAPTER 22

Tools to Shape Your Culture

by Nadya Khoja

Ping pong tables and "Scotch Fridays" don't lead to success and growth.

Sure, these are nice benefits to have, but in the long run, they will just lead to a more complacent staff—a group confused about what the actual values and goals of the business are.

What many CEOs and VPs struggle to accomplish is identifying what exactly "culture" means and why it's important. There are a few things you can do to start focusing on improving your culture and using it as a tool to boost productivity, find top talent, and accelerate growth.

Be Explicit about What Matters

Core values are essentially a deeper look into the behaviors of a company and specifically the behaviors that lead to success.

Jocelyn Goldfein of Zetta Venture Partners says, "culture is the behavior you reward and punish."

How often do new employees make their way into a company already understanding the culture? Not often. It takes time for new hires to get their bearings and fit in. What do they do instead? They look around and try to mimic what other people are doing—specifically, what the top performers are doing.

Here is an exercise you can do during your next team meeting. Ask everyone what it takes to be successful at your company. Write down the responses. These are the behaviors that your business rewards and, in turn, the values you promote. Next, make a list of these values and ask your team to describe what it means to demonstrate those values, using specific examples.

For example, Venngage has five main core values that make a great employee:

1. You own your job.
2. You reflect, plan, and act.
3. You continuously improve.
4. You are a team player.
5. You create great customer Ies.

Although these values describe *what* it is we look for in employees, they fail to address *how* to demonstrate each core value. It's extremely important that your staff understands the how, Ih is why you must go through each value and ask your team how they would demonstrate it. For instance, when I asked the marketing team how to "own their jobs" as marketers, they came up with the following list:

- Staying on top of trends in the industry and hot topics
- Knowing what strengths you bring to the team and capitalizing on that
- Being open to learning new things
- Taking accountability for your own actions
- Being proactive/taking initiative
- Presenting the company to others positively (brand evangelism)
- Striving to become a thought leader
- Staying on top of deadlines
- Constantly working towards becoming a well-rounded marketer

So, how do you get people to embody those behaviors?

Measure Values vs. Behavior

In Gino Wickman's book *Traction: Get a Grip on Your Business*, he talks about an evaluation process called "The People Analyzer." This process is, first and foremost, designed to clarify whether or not you have the right person in the right role. The secondary purpose is to identify if the members on your team do, in fact, demonstrate the company's core values.

Here is what it looks like:

Name	Own Your Job	Create Great Customer Experiences	Reflect, Plan, and Act	Continuous Improvement	Win Together, Lose Together
John	–	–	–	–	–
Linda	+/–	+/–	+/–	+/–	+/–
Alice	+	+	+	+	+

The scale is easy to follow. A minus sign means the person does not reflect that behavior, a plus sign means they do, and a plus/minus sign means that they kind of embody the value, but aren't where they should be.

Get Serious about Enforcing Culture

Every 30 days, use the people analyzer to "grade" each of your employees. If they underperform in a certain area, be sure that you bring up the issue. Let them know that you will check in again in 30 days. This is their first strike.

After Ir 30 days, if they are still underperforming, go over the issues once more during your one-on-one. What specifically are they doing wrong? Where are they falling short? Be specific. Then, give them Ir 30 days to get up to speed. This is strike two.

If after Ir 30 days the minus sign is still holding strong, it is unlikely that the employee will improve. This is the point when you should let them go. This is strike three.

Reward Embodying Culture

Like I mentioned before, new employees—or existing ones for that matter—will mimic good behavior. If they see that one particular employee gets along well with the boss, that their opinions are Is heard, and that they are awarded exciting opportunities, others will try to follow their patterns.

To clarify your culture and help others embody it, reward behaviors that reflect the culture. At Venngage, we give "shout outs" to A-players every week during our team meetings. For instance, if Alice took initiative to attend a meetup on growth marketing during the weekend, that is a prime example of demonstrating the core value of "continuous improvement."

Envision the Greater Goal

As a CEO, you have an agenda—a greater goal you want to achieve. What is that goal? I'll tell you now it shouldn't be revenue driven. Revenue should be a side effect of hitting that goal.

Some might assume that a CEO's goal is the mission statement of the company, but this is not entirely accurate. The mission statement is the company goal, but your goal as a CEO needs to be more personal. There's a more pointed question that might lead you towards better understanding what that goal is: How do you want to be remembered? What do you want the words on your tombstone to read?

It's important that you figure out the answer to this Ie it's what will guide the values that make up the culture of your company, and in turn, lead to your success. Culture can make or break a company. Do not be the person who puts your product above your culture. Instead, focus on providing meaning to the work your employees do.

PART III

THE HOW OF LEADERSHIP

CHAPTER 23

Four Things the New Leader of an Organization Should Do Right Away

by Tom Gimbel Mesh

C hanging leadership is an adjustment process for all concerned. How well the new leader and the current employees will interact is a source of concern on everyone's part, as are the cultural ramifications within the organization. It's a period of excitement, growing pains, and hope. As the incoming leader in an existing organization, it's largely up to you to take the first steps in easing the transition.

While earning the trust and loyalty of an entire organization is a challenge, there are four things an incoming leader can do right away to hit the ground running and earn support:

1. Get to Know All Levels of Staff

In some situations, new leadership can mean staff changes across the board. But in most cases, tenured staffers remain in place. The new head coach of a sports team can be great, but he has to start with the players the team already has on their roster. Focus on earning the trust and respect of those retained staff members.

United Airlines CEO Oscar Munoz is a great example of a new leader who came in and got to know people at all levels. He noticed "there was a high level of distrust and disengagement with employees" when he came in. That's not unusual. When new leadership takes over, some people may be skeptics at first.

Munoz revamped company morale in a grassroots way. He spent time in the maintenance hangar with the mechanics, and he stood on the tarmac with the baggage handlers; he showed he genuinely cared about the people who were working toward achieving the company vision. Such authenticity gets people re-engaged. It helps break down barriers between ranks and shows that the leader is one of the people. And often, the best and most innovative ideas will be the ones that come from the people with their ears to the ground every day.

2. Inspire Camaraderie

Even though Marissa Mayer's time at Yahoo! has been panned, what she attempted to do made strategic sense. She came under fire when she ended remote work and mandated employees to come into the office. The criticism made it seem like she was taking a personal stand against working remotely. She wasn't. It was about fixing a broken company culture. If the company had been succeeding when she took over, it would be a different story.

Mayer understood the importance of having people in close proximity to their bosses and colleagues. People need that fire in their seat that comes from the energy in a room full of people working together toward a common goal. It may mean having more people in the office more often, or in some cases, knocking down some of the partitions so that people are able to engage with one Ir. There are many ways to inspire camaraderie, Ih can be so important in a company's culture.

3. Hold People Accountable

Hold employees accountable. Encourage them to take owner-ship of their roles and speak up when they have opinions and ideas. Then, showcase the successes that come as a result.

I tell my staff all the time: If you speak up at work, you will have to do something to prove your thoughts and feelings are valid. It pushes you to act. Too often, people assume that someone else will figure it out. But often, they don't. Speaking up is not about complaining; it's about executing. Employees need to be part of the solution.

4. Identify the Superstars and Build on Them

Every leader has their own way of gauging top talent, but too often, it happens indirectly. For new leaders, there's a benefit to taking a staff inventory right away. Pay close attention and determine the key producers. It will take some time to get an accurate picture of people's abilities (the amount of time will depend on the size of the company), but putting in extra time to know the staff in the early phases will lay a foundation for identifying the key players the company needs to invest in and recruit again.

As you get a feel for the staff, make a three-column list. In one column, you have 3, 4, or maybe even 10 or 20 names (depending on the size of the company) of people you believe are the best performers. In the second column, list the most competent today. And in the third column, list who you believe has the most potential to be great. Each list will have mostly different names, but there will be rare cases where there is some overlap. These lists might change as you make more observations over time. The point is to have a visual running reference for those who needs more challenging work, extra attention, or corporate grandparenting. It's about making sure the company's future is in the best hands.

CHAPTER 24

Being a Trusted Leader: Knowing How to Grow Your Company

by Heather R. Huhman

The family-like environment of a new business can be a powerful thing. It allows both employees and leaders to come to work each day feeling as though they're there to make a difference. By being a team, employees feel the company is stronger.

"When I first started Overit, it was just a small marketing agency," recalls Dan Dinsmore, founder and CEO of Overit, in Albany, New York. "I was involved in everything and got to interact with employees on a daily basis."

But as startups begin to evolve, that relationship may be hard to maintain, as Dinsmore discovered. To take his company to the next level, he needed to hire middle managers to oversee operations. Doing that, however, created a distinct divide between him and his employees.

"It started to feel like an 'us vs. them' environment," Dinsmore pointed out. "That wasn't the kind of company I wanted to build."

To get things back on track, Dinsmore said he needed to rethink his company and how he could once again be a trusted leader. It took a lot of work to rebuild a culture of transparency and honesty.

Luckily, it's possible to avoid that "us vs. them" mentality. Here are four strategies for keeping your startup employees and leadership united:

1. Admit Your Mistakes

One of the hardest things for leaders to do is to own up when they are wrong. The feeling is that any mistake will be viewed as weakness or incompetence. But to be a trusted leader, being accountable for failure is a necessity.

"Right out of college, I was an assistant receptionist for a big-time entertainment executive in New York," recalled Kirsten Helvey, now the COO of Cornerstone OnDemand in Santa Monica, California. "One day, I got his lunch order wrong."

It wasn't long before Helvey's boss called her and screamed at her for the mistake. Despite the fact that any of his other assistants could have corrected the issue, he wanted to make sure she knew she'd messed up. "At that point," Helvey went on to say, "All trust was broken: his trust in my ability as his assistant and mine in his temperament as a manager."

Luckily, her boss had a change of heart. About 30 minutes later, he called Helvey back. He apologized for his behavior and said there was no excuse to speak to her that way. The incident turned into a life lesson Helvey uses now that she's part of the C-suite.

"It showed me that even if you're at the top, you can still mess up and damage the trust between you and your employees. But if you hold yourself accountable and make amends to the people your mistake has impacted, you can recover, grow, and even strengthen that relationship."

2. Delegate

As a leader, you may find it difficult to let go of control of any aspect of your company. But to be a trusted leader, being able to delegate is a must. Otherwise, employees may doubt their leader's capabilities.

"When I first hired employees for my small business, I found that it was challenging for me to let go of certain tasks and trust that my employees could handle them," said Rachel Beider, CEO and founder of Massage Williamsburg and Massage Greenpoint, in New York City. "I was used to doing everything myself and at a certain standard."

However, it wasn't long before her micromanaging began to take a toll. "I think it drove everyone a little crazy at first," Beider said. "We weren't being as productive as we should have been at that time."

Once she decided to take a step back, however, things began to run more smoothly. Her employees began to feel trusted, and she was able to concentrate on the company's growth and long-term goals.

To make delegating easier, take a moment and think: Is there anyone else who can Iy do this task? If the answer is yes, pass it on to that person and focus on big-picture strategies.

3. Empower Your Employees to Ask for Feedback

Things move fast at a growing startup. There is Is something to do, and sometimes, providing employees with feedback gets overlooked. But that causes them to feel forgotten by their leaders.

After working in a fast-paced company following college, Steffen Maier soon learned this lesson firsthand. Whenever his manager found time to give him feedback, months had typically passed since the project was completed. This time gap left him unsure of his own personal career progress.

"The interesting thing is that after I left my job to pursue a master's degree in strategic entrepreneurship, I was surprised to find that many of my peers had faced similar Ies," said Maier, now the cofounder of Impraise in New York City.

As a result, he and a few others teamed up to create Impraise, a platform designed to make it easy for employees to ask for and receive feedback. Using this or similar tools allows employees to continue to feel supported and connected with trusted leaders.

4. Put Trust above All Else

Never forget that a huge part of organizational trust is communication and honesty—without them, employees find it impossible to know where they stand. And that creates a division between those in the know and those who aren't.

"For us, success begins with trust," said Tom Morselli, senior vice president of people operations at PulsePoint, a programmatic advertising technology company based in New York City. "Trust in our leadership, trust in our mission, and trust among the team. It takes hard work and must be earned by 'walking the walk,' keeping promises, following through, and aligning one's leadership style with the company's core values."

All of that happens through clear and consistent communication at all levels of the company. Luckily, there are multiple, easy-to-use tools that help keep teams connected. One option is Simpplr, a platform that offers organizations an intranet that promotes and maintains productive information-sharing. It gives employees access to company news and a way to formally and informally interact with one other.

Employees should also recognize, however, that all that talk needs follow-up.

"The most empathetic and best-intended talk is hollow if it isn't followed by action," Morselli pointed out. "Trust erodes quickly if you consistently fail to meet your commitments."

CHAPTER 25

How to Build a Great Workplace—for Free

by Jeffrey Hayzlett

Everyone is familiar with the culture that companies like Apple and Google have built in Silicon Valley. But not everyone can afford that "rock star" type of culture—and some might not even want it.

In Webster's dictionary, culture is "the integrated pattern of human knowledge, belief, and behavior that depends upon the capacity for learning and transmitting knowledge to succeeding generations."

In your workplace, culture is the everyday reality of organizational life. It is not the mission statement, your balance sheets, or even the employee handbook. The culture is what we do, what we say, the way we behave, and the way we treat each other. That encompasses everything from our products to our customers to our communities and even to ourselves.

As entrepreneurs, we left corporate America for a number of reasons, one of them being our dissatisfaction with the company's culture. We left to create something that fit our dreams, our persona, and our vision—our perfect corporate utopia.

How can we as business owners do that?

1. Start with Purpose

In the beginning, all that matters is building something great and lasting. When the head count is in the single digits, people discuss their soon-to-be culture around the table. Problems are still simple, and communication is direct. But as the company starts growing, communication becomes more sporadic (or non-existent), and consensus becomes harder to reach.

To avoid that scenario, have a purpose when you establish your new company's culture. To create that purpose, understand the "why" of the operation. What (or whom) does your business serve? Whatever IIswer is, it should be authentic, inspirational, and aspirational. Companies with a strong purpose are well liked Ie they feel different (think Ikea or Apple).

Just don't think about copying these giants; no one likes a copycat. Instead, do what's right for your company. Think about what inspires you, and then execute it.

2. Create a Common Language, Values, and Standards

For a culture to be successful, those at your company must speak the same language and be on the same page about what your values are. This common language needs to be understood by everyone in the company—from the CEO down to the mail room worker. Write down those values. This makes them tangible, an essential element to make your culture withstand the test of time.

You must also have a common set of values—Ih are just your company's principles—and a common set of standards to measure how your principles are being upheld.

Only when you have aligned your language, values, and standards will you have a cohesive culture. Cohesiveness should be your end goal. It might seem tempting to employ a number of stopgaps along the way, but that's only a short-term solution.

In order to create a long-lasting culture everyone understands, that culture will need to adapt as the company grows. Your core values are your constant staples, but the overall culture needs to be malleable enough to acclimate to different employees and changing times.

3. Lead by Example

A culture is shaped by how a company's leaders act. Every leader needs to internally and externally reflect the company's values and be its strongest advocates. They shouldn't recite the mission statement as a solution to everything, but should exemplify what the company stands for.

Think about the Virgin brand and how Richard Branson embodies everything the company wants people to see them as: fun, bold, brash, and spirited. Leaders who exemplify incredible passion for what they do and have an exemplary work ethic are the main source of inspiration for other employees and those who want to join the company.

As a leader, you need to lead by example and be radically transparent. It won't matter one iota if you think you have a great culture, yet your employees don't trust you. Being transparent, even when that's difficult, will go a long way toward preserving the culture you originally envisioned.

4. Identify Imbassadors

Every company has them: employees who live, eat, and breathe your culture and help everyone else understand who you are as a company and what you stand for. These employees are your biggest advocates Ie they love the company almost as much as you do—they are your cheerleaders.

This type of employee is an invaluable asset. Once you identify who your cheerleaders are, ask them what they like about the current culture, what they don't like, and why culture matters to them. That will help you gauge whether you should stay the course or make a few changes to the current culture.

The role of these ambassadors doesn't diminish with time. On the contrary, their role increases as your company grows and, in the end, gives you a competitive advantage. Why? Ie customers will remember those who are positive and knowledgeable about the company (or brand) they represent.

5. Communicate Often and Honestly

Integrity has been defined as "doing the right thing, even when nobody's watching." Whatever you do, you must Is demand that everyone in your company adhere to being truthful and approach everything with the utmost integrity. Failure to comply is not an option.

Part of being truthful as a leader is being completely honest about your strengths, weaknesses, and biases. It's pretty easy to boast about your talents, but don't think for a second you don't have any weaknesses—you do. This doesn't apply only to leadership, but to everyone.

As a leader, you must Is communicate your values explicitly and continuously, internally and externally. Every employee must understand the culture and why it's important to preserve it. Self-awareness and communication will be essential when your culture isn't going all that well. Culture doesn't have to be a neatly wrapped package, but your communication and truthfulness must never waver. If people can't trust you, you don't have a leg to stand on.

6. Treat People Right

As a CEO or company leader, you need to treat your employees well. Otherwise, the culture you're trying to establish won't be of much use to you if you have a high turnover rate.

When you're thinking about hiring new employees, spend time screening for character rather than skill. Don't get me wrong: An impressive resume is something to be proud of, and it's important. But if your character is questionable, you're not a good fit for my company. Skills can be learned, but it's much harder to cultivate a good attitude and character.

Hiring someone with impressive skills and a bad attitude is a sure-fire way to sabotage your own culture, but once you've hired the right people, treat them right. Once you find someone with the right cultural fit, do everything in your power to develop them, and help that person scale.

You don't have to spend a fortune on an in-house sushi chef and a state-of-the-art office to create a great workplace. All six of these steps don't cost anything, and yet I know many people who would willingly trade their rock star work environment for a job in a company that embodied these traits.

CHAPTER 26

How to Motivate Your Team Members by Putting Their Needs First

by Jennifer Biry

L eadership styles are like fingerprints. They leave an unmistakable mark on whatever they touch and are unique to each individual. And while we don't get to choose our fingerprints, we do get to choose how we lead those around us.

I've had the opportunity to see a wide variety of leadership styles. I gained most of my Ie working at large corporations, but for 20 years, I've been married to an entrepreneur who showed me the challenges that come with running your own business. I've learned that no matter the size of your organization or the scope of your role at work, you can be a leader. But deciding Ih leadership style is right for you takes time.

For me, servant leadership has proved to be the most effective approach.

Here are five steps you can take to be a servant leader.

1. Be Humble

Ego plays a huge role in your leadership style. I believe confidence balanced with humility is a recipe for leadership success. Don't let personal pride get in the way of trying something new. Is assume someone in the room is smarter than you. You'll learn more that way.

I see this kind of humility on a regular basis from Cynt Marshall, former chief diversity officer of AT&T. She has an incredibly demanding job that requires a significant investment of time for all her internal and external commitments. But when you talk to her, she gives you 100 percent of her attention and makes it clear that you're her number-one priority at that moment. She constantly uplifts her team by celebrating their great work, and she goes out of her way to make them look good. As a result, people follow her without question.

2. Trust Your Team

In most cases, you hired the people on your team Ie you were confident in their abilities. Trust your intuition and give up a little control. Creativity flourishes in an open environment, so don't constrict your employees by involving yourself in smaller decisions that they can handle. Giving your team room to grow will benefit everyone in the long run.

I was on the receiving end of this kind of trust when I was a CFO supporting AT&T's call centers. Our boss tasked us with trying to figure out how to reduce the number of customer transfers between the centers. After a week of analyzing procedures, we put forth our recommendation. At the end of our presentation, our boss told us he knew a solution from the get-go; he just wanted to hear the ideas we came up with when we worked as a team to solve the problem. He was pleased to find that we uncovered other possibilities he hadn't yet considered. Encouraging us to have ownership over the solution was a powerful example for me of what it means to truly trust your team.

3. Lead from the Back of the Room

If you're a supervisor, don't think you need to be front and center all the time. It's important to listen intently—at least twice as often as you speak. Create an environment where all voices and ideas are heard, and most important, give your team room to spread their wings. For example, if they did the work, they should present the results.

By doing this, you can serve as your employees' guide instead of dictating their every move. Let the team lead themselves and be willing to accept mistakes or failures. This will encourage risk-taking and help your employees learn how to manage similar challenges in the future.

4. Set a Broad Vision

Servant leadership isn't about being the nice guy; it's about delivering great results. Anyone who's worked with me will tell you I have high standards and push my team to excel. However, instead of managing each task, I inspire my team by helping them see that what they do is a critical component of a greater cause. Over the years, I found that people will work even harder if they believe in what they're doing.

Many times In my career, I've been asked to lead cost-cutting projects. As you might imagine, those aren't the most popular assignments to work on. So, I Is try to create a broader vision. As opposed to tasking my team with cutting costs, I ask that they look for ways to increase earnings per share enough to elevate the stock price. People are Is more motivated by seeing the impact of their work on a broader scale.

5. Develop Future Leaders

One of my most important responsibilities is to develop the next generation of leaders. As it turns out, it's also what I enjoy most about my job. When I mentor someone, I ask them in return to pull five more leaders forward with them. If you don't have a mentoring program in your organization, set one up. Your employees will develop stronger relationships and share insights and skills. And the emphasis you put on their professional growth will make them feel more valued.

Practicing these behaviors will bolster your team's success and foster an environment of respect across your organization. You'll be seen as a leader, not as a boss.

Take some time to step back, assess your leadership style, and look for ways to improve. Is there room for more humility? Can you relinquish some control? And are you personally invested in every employee's success?

Ask yourself these questions, and then make it a priority to empower your team. Once you start "walking the walk" of servant leadership, you'll see your people shine.

CHAPTER 27

Creating Space for Introverts to Flex Their Superpower

by Pratik Dholakiya

I n the business world, we've all heard and read classic euphemisms which imply that success is directly tied to the quality of being extroverted. In fact, facets like high performance and business potential are directly (and stereotypically) attributed to this quality.

But introverts have their own contributions to make. These people are characteristically defined as shy, quiet, passive, or antisocial (though those qualities may not be unilaterally true for every introvert you employ). And these personality attributes make introverts highly adept at strategic planning, creative thinking, and problem-solving skills that are an asset to any team.

Of course, as the company leader, you must know how to enable those skills. And that requires a leadership and organizational approach that provides accommodation without objectifying or singling out an introverted individual. From

147

the socializing that goes on in your office space to the dynamic that emerges at team meetings, your managers can potentially impact employee retention for the better by adopting a tailored approach to your introverted staff.

Identifying Introverts in the Workplace

The scale of introversion is not always about extremes; an individual may have many extroverted tendencies, but still identify internally as an introvert. This can make it rather difficult for managers to identify members of the team who have different needs to help them perform to expectations.

Psychometric testing is a cornerstone of recruitment and human resource management and is a reliable method of determining the degree of introversion and best practices for a balanced team environment.

Tip

The Myers Briggs Personality Inventory is also a valuable resource for managers and human resource professionals and can provide essential management insights.

Open Workspaces

Globally, there exists a trend that is being driven more by economics and less by employee need: the open-office layout. As commercial business space becomes more expensive, and as businesses grow, moving to a larger building may not be a practical solution. Enter options that help make the most of existing workspaces: telecommuting and the open-office plan.

The problem is that open-office layouts do not work for many introverts. Characteristically, these employees are pensive, deep thinkers who require a place that is quiet and free of stimulation and distractions to provide their best work. Open offices hinder concentration by eliminating that private buffer, and in these settings, noise becomes a problem that prevents introverts from focusing effectively.

In terms of team dynamics, open-office settings also inhibit the development of close personal relationships between introverts and their colleagues. Uncomfortable with conversations that are audible by "everyone around them," introverts are likely to avoid personal conversations during the workday. They'll avoid those brief, friendly interactions that enhance communication among co-workers because those interchanges lack the privacy and sense of safety for having a conversation.

Introverts have a lower tolerance to excessive stimuli (which distracts and creates stress for them), and they prefer face-to-face engagements with smaller groups of people.

Tip

Moving to an open-work-space plan may be inevitable, but creating "withdrawal space" for work is essential to productivity (and retention). Ensure that you incorporate small pods or offices that can be used by individual staff who wish to retreat to a quiet area.

Feedback

Part of any small departmental or large organizational meeting is the prompt to share feedback and ideas. The first people to speak up naturally are extroverted members of your team, who feel more than comfortable being heard in front of a crowd. Extroverts are also better able to process criticism in front of others, which makes them virtually fearless about sharing ideas, comments, or problems with their team.

The average introvert, meanwhile, may be frustrated in a public feedback situation. As the deep thinkers in your organization, introverted personnel are not short on ideas or suggestions for creative problem-solving. However, if the only opportunity that is provided occurs within a very public setting, you can count on your introverted staff to avoid sharing. Not only will an organization miss the value of their contributions, but introverts may feel diminished in value and excluded from the team.

Tip

Extroverts tend to dominate most meetings, and while their enthusiasm and contributions are important, it is equally important that leadership professionals moderate that engagement to prevent other members from feeling overwhelmed.

At the end of any small or large meeting, ensure that you offer a method for introverts to submit their feedback, comments, or ideas in writing. This gesture can be as simple as encouraging staff who did not have an opportunity to share to send a summary email with their questions, comments, or ideas. Being open to contribution by a variety of methods helps introverts feel less overshadowed by more outspoken colleagues.

Body Language and Work Preferences

It's easy to determine in most cases how extroverts are feeling about a situation, considering these people exhibit expressive body language and visual cues. Introverts, however, can demonstrate a flat affect that may be misinterpreted by both management and extroverted team members.

An introvert, for example, may require more time to formulate an idea because of their personality style. However, many studies have demonstrated that more than 70 percent of individuals with high-functioning intellects are introverted.

The additional time that an employee takes to articulate a response or to provide an idea is frequently the precursor to innovation. It is not a lack of responsiveness, but rather an intense ability to handle complex issues and provide results. Given the time to matriculate and organize their ideas, introverts provide highly detailed plans and solutions.

Tip

Team-building exercises and personality sensitivity training can be valuable ways to increase awareness and combat stereotypes and assumptions. By identifying both extroverts and introverts as a performance asset, both groups can work cohesively (and respectfully) within your organization.

Negative Feedback

In some research studies, it's been reported that extroverts are adept at managing public criticism far better than introverts. While introversion is not synonymous with shyness or weakness (despite stereotypes), these people find the spotlight to be a stressful place to be in social and professional settings. An extrovert may, therefore, be able to process a reprimand in front of other colleagues and recover quickly, while an introvert may Ie significant stress and personal offense from the same feedback.

Tip

For important feedback or performance-review meetings, managers (whenever possible) should communicate privately with introverted colleagues or employees. Not only will this eliminate a deeply humiliating Ie for the introvert, but it will also allow them the safety and reassurance to respond to questions.

Organizations that understand the ways in Ih both personality types offer value and those that are willing to pivot leadership approaches, depending on whether an employee is an extrovert or introvert, can anticipate a more harmonious environment, increased employee engagement, and long-term retention of talented professionals.

CHAPTER 28

Six Things You Must Do to Effectively Manage Remote Workers

by Tricia Sciortino

W e've heard it all before. Remote workers are picking up steam at unprecedented levels. According to the U.S. Bureau of Labor Statistics, almost one-quarter of employed people perform some, or all, of their work from their kitchen table, home office, or back porch. And fewer business leaders question that virtual work promotes cost savings, ramps up performance, and deepens employee retention.

But, a major question remains: How can we onboard new offsite talent to ensure they stay the course, perform according to corporate values, produce as expected, and integrate well with other distributed team members? Perhaps some of these unresolved and persistent issues explain why companies like Honeywell and Charter Communications have banned work-from-home options. But there are many, many businesses starting out with a virtual model from day one in addition to companies that have started to incorporate remote team members into their organizations. For these reasons, it's important to keep the conversation about virtual workplaces alive.

At BELAY, where I serve as COO, we have a number of full-timers who work from home, along with a multitude of contractors who do likewise across the U.S. As you might imagine, I've learned lots of lessons about hiring and holding on to remote teams over the years. And I know that early experiences and training can really make a difference.

Here's how:

1. *Aim for consistency—from day one.* When all new employees are onboarding together, their introduction to the company begins from a basis of common understanding. And from this accord, they grow closer to the business and to each other through the shared experience of orientation. New employee training can be delivered remotely, yet remain a collective process. Self-study programs, inclusive of videos, online communities, digital assessments, and more, give newcomers an opportunity to engage in content, communicate with others, and learn at the same time.

2. *Love technology.* Technology is a virtual company's best friend. We depend on it for security, cloud-based collaboration, daily communication, project management, and more. But it's also a must-have in the toolbox for a company with remote employees. Not only do technologies support business needs, but they also enable visual communication, promote auditory engagement, and even allow for employees to test new skills, such as serving as presenters during online meetings and events.

3. *Know when to pick up the phone.* Virtual teams rely on technology and embrace its capabilities for connection, access, and collaboration. But one of the most important lessons I've learned is that back-and-forth emails mean the message—whatever it may be—is not getting through. Someone needs to pick up the phone or get on a webcam meeting. Online dashboards and communication platforms have their place, for sure. However, old-fashioned talking cannot be replaced. Speaking with each other—and seeing one another, even if remotely—clarifies matters, prevents missteps, and resonates with so much of what still works for us as real people.

4. *Get together—regularly.* There's no absolute one-size-fits-all standard about how often teams should meet in person. But it helps to ingrain face-to-face gatherings into the operational DNA of an organization. At the very least, when the central, or corporate, players can convene on a routine basis, it helps to reinforce purpose and unity. If strategy and budget allow, it can only be beneficial to take this practice to the next level, creating ways for all team members to meet, greet, network, and learn together in the same physical space. This is especially true in the early days of their employment.

5. *Check in, with diligence and dedication.* It's important for new employees to maintain a connection with their managers and the broader corporate mission. One way to foster and preserve this is through regularly occurring feedback. While impromptu check-ins can be

beneficial, it's more intentional and meaningful to ensure performance meetings are a permanent fixture on HR's and supervisors' calendars. This can mean convening after the first 30 days, having weekly one-on-ones, and establishing other ways to assess expectations and performance by employee and employer alike.

6. *Learn from the same hymnals.* My company requires new employees to read the same three books. We selected these titles based on how well they reflect our corporate culture and align with our business personality. Sharing in this reading exercise sets the tone for how our team members should operate and perform on the job, while also providing them with new, relevant insights for their own personal and professional development, too.

Working remotely is no longer a new business trend or for the more cutting-edge companies. The latest technology has not only made it easy, but continues to advance the possibilities. To enhance your use of technology, it is essential that remote employees have the necessary tools and know how to use them. Training, tutorials, and support are integral so off-site employees do not feel lost or disconnected when they are 5 or 500 miles away.

It is important to recognize that technology, notwithstanding the human element, is still a factor and will hopefully remain as such. Actual phone conversations, get-togethers, and in-person meetings help humanize the business culture and unite those involved. Phone conversations should not become a lost art, nor should face-to-face discussions. Camaraderie, enthusiasm, and the team concept cannot be understated—even in a remote working environment.

The best way to work with remote employees is not to let them feel removed from the company.

CHAPTER 29

Increase Accountability without Breathing Down People's Necks

by Karim Abouelnaga

One of the toughest balances to achieve within an organization is between building a culture that gives people space while maintaining an environment of accountability. The line between managing and micromanaging is very fine and in some cases blurry. At Practice Makes Perfect, we've operated with an unlimited vacation policy for almost a year now. We close our offices for every federal holiday and have a compulsory two days off that everyone has to take per quarter to recharge. In order to operate with this level of flexibility, we have to ensure that controls are in place so that work gets done. More importantly, we don't want to stifle creativity.

Here is how we ensure accountability without breathing down everyone's neck:

Create Annual Goals

Every year, we set three to five goals that everyone in the entire company rallies behind. At the end of the year, those are the only goals that matter. We know we are done with our planning when we can respond "yes" to the following question: If we looked back at the end of the year and this is all that we accomplished, would we be satisfied? A resounding, "yes," is required before we settle. It is also important to limit yourself to five. If you have too many priorities, then nothing becomes a priority.

Develop Quarterly Objectives

Every department leader sets objectives that stem from the annual goals we set for the company. Each department will also set departmentwide objectives. The objectives are then assigned to managers within the department who are responsible for delegating and project managing throughout the course of the quarter. The managers are accountable for the objectives, and their teams are responsible for delivering on them.

As a company, we also have a quarterly critical number (one key priority that can be measured and tracked that will move the company forward). The critical number is the most important priority for everyone within the company. We tie incentives during our quarterly celebration to our level of success at achieving our critical number. At the end of the quarter, we reflect on the critical number from the previous quarter and then share the critical number for the following quarter.

In an effort to document our journey and increase transparency, I also write a quarterly letter where I reflect on the things that went well and the things that didn't go as planned throughout the quarter. It also allows me to solicit help and anticipate what we have ahead of us for the following quarter.

Focus on Monthly Targets

Every month, we update a Key Performance Indicator (KPI) dashboard that is managed by the executive team. Once it is populated, we reflect on it with the company leadership team, and then, I put together an email to the entire company that includes the dashboard and comments on how we are doing toward our annual goals. This creates an incredible amount of accountability and transparency within the organization. Everyone has access to this document, and they easily see how we are managing our expenses, how much revenue we're bringing in, and what our company's burn rate is at that given moment. The executive team then holds a monthly town hall for people to bring up any questions or concerns they may have.

Have Weekly Emails

Toward the end of every week, we ask everyone in the organization to send a brief email to their manager. The email has three sections: challenges, successes, and a third section for anything the manager or company should start/stop/continue. If the person manages a budget, they also update any revenue or expense numbers. This should take no longer than 15 minutes. They are meant to be short and sweet, with the purpose of really shedding light on key items.

Once a week, every manager will also have a 10- to 20-minute check-in with their direct reports. Though they are fairly unstructured, they are opportunities to talk through the challenges in a weekly report, check in on any needs a team member may have in order to carry out their job, and discuss professional development opportunities. When we check in, I like to speak with my direct reports about the items I keep on a running list occurring throughout the week.

Do Daily Check-Ins

Every morning at 9:05 A.M., we have a group huddle. Everyone present in the office (we're 15 people now; if we were 20, we'd split in half) forms a circle, and they come prepared to share the most significant thing that happened the day before, the most important thing (just one) that they will accomplish that day, and whether or not they foresee anything slowing them down. This usually takes us between seven and ten minutes. It also provides us an opportunity to share any important companywide announcements as they come up instead of trying to create a meeting with a long agenda or sending a handful of emails. For people who have a 9 A.M. meeting or are working from home, we have an organization huddle channel on Slack. The daily huddles allow us to collaborate and troubleshoot potential bottlenecks before they arise.

From annual goals to daily check-ins, you want to maintain a strong sense of purpose and of communication so that nobody feels unsure of their role in the organization. This is how we hold people accountable. Of course, the schedule will differ based on the logistics of each business, especially with people working from remote locations. The key is to have ongoing accountability without, as noted earlier, breathing down people's necks.

CHAPTER 30

Feedback That
Builds Culture

by Sujan Patel

I n the early days of her consultancy career, IBM performance marketing expert Jackie Bassett was assigned to a project that, as she wrote, she "didn't like very much." She was obliged to work crazy hours alongside a demoralized team with minimal instruction on the expectations of her role.

Although Bassett knew deep down that her performance wasn't up to scratch, no one said anything. It wasn't until her written performance evaluation—handed to her more than a month after the project ended—that she realized her superiors were unhappy with her work.

Bassett was left wondering, *Why didn't [they] say anything?*

Sadly, this is far from an isolated incident. It's not unusual for companies to provide scheduled feedback—such as when a project wraps up, or during a yearly review—yet fail to offer it when it's needed most and is most valuable: in real time.

Don't reserve feedback for "special occasions" like yearly reviews or the point at which something's gone wrong or spectacularly right. A simple "great job on xyz today" will go a long way toward boosting morale and creating a workplace in which feedback becomes part of the culture.

In fact, employees who receive regular feedback have been shown to work harder, be more engaged, and offer greater loyalty to their employers. The most successful companies have built a strong culture of feedback by making it a normal, everyday part of company life.

What are the best practices in these places?

Don't Put Too Much Stock in Performance Reviews

In an interview, Bill Sims, the author of *Green Beans & Ice Cream,* described how Microsoft had ended the use of a system known as "forced rankings." Part of performance reviews, forced rankings used a scoring system to identify the best- and worst-performing employees. The worst-performing employees might then be fired.

The problem with such a system (aside from its glaring brutality) is that performance reviews tend to focus on isolated examples of each employee's work. They're often carried out by top-level management with little, if any, direct contact with their employees' day-to-day performance. Instead, those managers rely on third-party reports from lower management and team leaders.

In short: Performance reviews are ineffective at improving performance.

Instead, the way to go is to empower and encourage those who work directly with your staff. In this way, you can appraise and praise employees' work as it happens.

Separate Positive and Negative Feedback

A popular management strategy is to cushion the blow of negative feedback by wrapping it in positivity. This is more commonly known as the "sandwich approach."

At first glance, the sandwich approach seems logical. It certainly feels like the kinder way of delivering bad news, but in the long run, it devalues positive feedback. If you need to address poor performance, focus on the issue at hand. Likewise, offer positive feedback when it's called for. Don't ever "save it" in order to soften its bad-news component. Research has shown that aspects of both positive and negative feedback are best shared as soon as possible.

Give More Good Feedback Than Bad

Both positive and negative feedback are very important. Positive feedback helps boost staff morale while negative feedback allows you to address problems head-on. Both forms of feedback serve to improve performance.

That said, a staff member receiving so much negative feedback that it outweighs the positive will understandably start to feel its brunt. If this happens, chances are there are one of two issues at play:

1. A genuine problem with the staff member's performance
2. A problem with management's approach to feedback

The first example is a separate issue unlikely to be resolved solely by feedback of any sentiment. The second example is the fault of management, which needs to overhaul its approach to ensure that positive feedback significantly outweighs the negative. How "significantly" should that be?

Research conducted by academic expert Emily Heaphy and consultant Marcial Losada in 2013 found that the average ratio of positive to negative comments for the highest-performing teams included in the study was 5.6.

That is, for every negative comment, there were nearly six positive ones.

They Use Trust as the Bedrock of Feedback

An effective culture of feedback has to be built on trust. If your staff members don't trust one another—or even you—how can you expect them to take feedback seriously?

To get around this, Shopify CEO Tobi Lütke implemented a system called the "trust battery." He's explained that the trust battery is,

> charged at 50 percent when people are first hired. And then every time you work with someone at the company, the trust battery between the two of you is either charged or discharged, based on things like whether you deliver on what you promise.

The concept stems from the fact that humans already work that way; the battery simply serves as a metaphor. It helps to strengthen the impact of another system that's unique to Shopify: an internal wiki that openly displays each employee's strengths and weaknesses. The wiki helps accelerate the process of learning about colleagues and how they work best (and how best to work with them). It's a great idea, but one that can only work under a culture of complete openness and trust.

It also explains why Google executive Larry Page can get away with "bursting into a room and making a big show of announcing that a set of ads sucked."

Most execs would terrify their employees with such an outburst, but Google has spent so long building an open, communicative culture of trust that in this context, it works.

In all these examples, feedback is embedded in the companies' overall culture. Just as importantly, feedback supports and reinforces their cultures instead of demoralizing their employees or eroding the workplace environment.

Can your business say the same?

CHAPTER 31

How a CEO Can Fix Corporate Culture

by Shellye Archambeau

When corporate culture makes the news, it's usually for all the wrong reasons. United Airlines has become almost infamous for its treatment of passengers from the viral hit "United Breaks Guitars" to the viral video of the doctor being dragged down the aisle.

But for every company whose culture results in these types of newsworthy stories, there is a Southwest Airlines, famous for its employees-first mantra and spirit of inclusiveness that inspire teams to go the extra mile for customers. There is a Quicken Loans, whose "isms" or cultural values—like "simplicity is genius" and "yes before no"—have led the company to become one of the fastest growing online mortgage lenders, not to mention one of *Fortune* magazine's top 10 best companies to work for.

We could examine what's wrong with United's culture (or any of dozens of companies famous for their awful employee engagement practices). But a good company culture isn't just about avoiding doing the wrong things; it's also about doing the right things.

In successful companies, culture goes beyond free yoga classes, gourmet meals, and other perks. It's about creating a work environment based on shared values and principles—ideals so deeply embedded in the organization's DNA that they become intrinsic to daily decisions. It is about building a business where people can collectively thrive and grow. It's about an environment where people are driven to do good work—better work—that translates into higher customer satisfaction and better performance. Culture is the glue that binds a company together. As with most things in a business, it starts at the top.

What can a CEO do to improve corporate culture?

Listen More, Talk Less

When you're busy running a company, it's easy to miss what's happening on the frontlines. Would employees at Wells Fargo have created those millions of fake bank and credit card accounts if executives had actually listened to their employees, and understood the pressures that they were under to meet sales targets? Employees live the organization's culture every day, and if something is not quite right, they are the first ones to know—which is why it so important to tune in to what they are saying.

Website design startup Squarespace keeps its finger on the pulse of the organization by maintaining a flat, open culture where there are minimal levels of management between staff and executives. This gives employees the confidence to voice their opinions freely.

Encouraging open dialog is important. At MetricStream, I keep a stuffed elephant in my office. It is meant as a reminder that I encourage team members to "put the elephants on the table." You could conduct surveys to collect employee feedback, talk to your staff face-to-face, or establish hotlines where people can report grievances and concerns without fear of being targeted.

As you listen, pay attention to the subtext and non-verbal cues. Employees might be telling you one thing, but their expressions and gestures might be signifying the opposite. Are they afraid to speak the truth? If so, what does that say about your culture? Similarly, when sending out surveys, take note of how many people respond or how many questions they skipped. At team meetings, observe how people interact. Do they look engaged? Do they ask questions? These signals provide important insights into your organization's culture and its alignment with corporate values.

Reward employees for speaking up and raising issues. Invite them to challenge your thoughts and bring diverse ideas and opinions to the table. When employees feel that they are being heard and know their concerns are noted, they will be more engaged, productive, and innovative.

Make Collaboration the Core of Your Culture

At the 2016 Rio Olympics, the Japanese 4x100 meters relay team pulled off an unexpected victory when it defeated North American sprinting legends to win the silver. None of the four

Japanese men by themselves were as fast as America's Justin Gatlin or Canada's Andre De Grasse. However, what they lacked in speed, they made up for in teamwork and seamless baton changes that ultimately gave them the winning edge.

Noted leadership expert Ken Blanchard once said, "None of us is as smart as all of us." Effective leaders understand this concept. They know that the best corporate cultures are created when people work as one unit towards common goals and values—when individual contributions come together to drive collective achievements.

However, fostering a spirit of collaboration in today's scattered, global organizations can be challenging. Many leaders limit collaboration to specific projects rather than viewing it as the bedrock of a successful organization. There are others who understand that one of the most basic human needs is to belong; when employees feel they're a valued member of a team that collaborates towards a meaningful purpose, they tend to be more innovative, high-performing, and satisfied.

Collaboration doesn't happen by accident, though. It takes a strong, sustained strategy and roadmap. Begin by helping employees realize the importance of collaboration—not only in achieving the organization's objectives—but also in fulfilling their own unique potential. Create a work environment of trust and respect where employees are free to express themselves. Invite them to work across silos with other teams and functions. Establish metrics that can measure and improve the level of collaboration.

Embrace the idea that "the whole is greater than the sum of its parts."

Encourage Risk-Taking

As someone who has spent much of her life taking risks, both as an individual and as the CEO of a company, I've learned that the most successful businesses are those unafraid to take chances. YouTube CEO Susan Wojcicki put it best when she said, "Life doesn't always present you with the perfect opportunity at the perfect time... Opportunities—the good ones—they're messy and confusing and hard to recognize. They're risky. They challenge you."

The only way to realize these opportunities is to establish a culture of risk-taking where employees across the organization are empowered to experiment and challenge the status quo. At MetricStream, one of our biggest innovations yet—the M7 GRC platform and apps—is the cumulative result of teams across the organization pushing the boundaries of technology to boldly go where few, if any, companies have gone before.

A strong culture of risk-taking is particularly important in a world that is constantly changing. If you want to innovate, transform, and disrupt, your employees have to take those leaps of faith. It starts with walking the talk: when employees see their leaders taking smart risks, they will follow suit.

You also need informed decision-making. Employees have to understand the risks they're taking. Encourage them to spend time measuring and analyzing the possible risks of their ideas so that they are prepared for the outcomes. Establish milestones, check-posts, and controls to ensure the risks don't spin out of control. Let employees know it's ok if things don't always work out.

When Google's much hyped Wave failed, then-CEO Eric

Schmidt told reporters, "Remember, we celebrate our failures. This is a company where it's absolutely ok to try something that's very hard, have it not be successful, and take the learning from that."

Culture is not something that just happens. Like anything worthwhile, it takes time, effort, and commitment. Take a leaf out of Asana's book. The tech company treats culture as a product that, like any app or software, requires careful design, testing, and debugging in endless iterations. Representatives from across the company meet regularly to take stock of corporate values and identify new ways to embed them. They also collect user feedback about what's working well and what is not. Unsurprisingly, the company was recently named among *Entrepreneur*'s best company cultures of 2017.

At the end of the day, companies like Asana know that culture is not just a "nice-to-have." It is as important as the product or service you're selling because when you have a robust, cohesive culture, you have happy employees. And when you have happy employees, you have higher productivity, happier customers, and stronger profits.

CHAPTER 32

The Easy Way to Improve Employee Engagement

by Matthew Baker

Employers take note: you're not holding the attention or interest of your employees. Think you're an exception to the rule? Think again. Seventy percent of American employees report being disengaged at work and three out of four are currently looking for a new job or are open to new opportunities.

While there is something to be said for options and hedging the risk of potential layoffs, this means more than half of your workforce is not passionate about what they're doing or committed to your organization.

Disengaged employees are doing a huge disservice to every aspect of your business. Research suggests they negatively affect everything from team morale to productivity to your bottom line.

While this paints a dreary picture, the good news is companies can take steps toward boosting employee engagement.

Traditional efforts include internal mobility programs, employee wellness initiatives, and appropriately rewarding behavior. But these can be a drain on resources and cost a lot of money. So, what's the cost-effective secret to improving employee engagement?

Building and maintaining a values-based culture.

A Culture Rooted in Values

Workplace culture is often misunderstood, and many measure it by the number of nap rooms and ping-pong tables. However, at its core, a successful culture is a system of shared beliefs and behaviors members of the workplace use to interact with one another.

Values capture what an organization believes is most important to the way it operates, such as teamwork, creativity, or diversity. Values are open to interpretation and, above all, dogmatic. A values-based culture exists when employees associate meaning to their behaviors based on specific company values.

Not sure if you have a values-based culture? Ask a few of your employees about a challenging decision they faced and which beliefs helped them reach a decision. Did they behave according to their own personal values? Financial goals? Emotional attachment? Or was the decision attributed to your company's values?

Values Set Boundaries and Provide Flexibility

A values-based culture relies on employee autonomy and empowerment to function. An individual is much more likely to drive better results when they feel ownership over their work. Values provide clear boundaries, but the space inside the boundaries is for exploration and innovation, allowing employees more freedom to shape the work they're doing.

The exercise of making decisions within a values-based culture fosters engagement. Conversely, making decisions solely based on a set of workflows, processes, and calculations requires intelligence and attention to detail. But frankly, it's boring and doesn't adequately capture and sustain the attention and interest of employees.

Large and small companies can benefit from a values-based culture. Moreover, the values from one organization to the next can be completely different.

A Look at Values–Based Cultures

McKinsey & Company, named Top 25 Places to Work, is a management consulting firm with more than 10,000 employees across 100 offices globally. The firm has three governing values:

- Adhere to the highest professional standards
- Improve our clients' performance significantly
- Create an unrivaled environment for exceptional people

One of the ways McKinsey & Company reinforces its values-based culture is an annual event called "Values Day." On this day, each office sets aside time to discuss what the values mean, including role-playing scenarios where the values are tested in challenging situations.

Another company that practices values-based culture is FreshBooks, a software company with 250 employees based in Toronto, Canada. The company has nine core values: passion, ownership, respect, change, honesty, fun, empathy, strive, and trust.

To bring these values to life, FreshBooks hosts an annual company retreat in honor of the values called PORCHFEST (the acronym is based on the first letter of each value) and offers an ongoing program called "Values Cards" encouraging employees to nominate each other for a gift card when their behavior epitomizes one of the values. One card, for example, read, "Samantha recently exhibited the value of Change by embracing a last-minute detour in the launch calendar that resulted in more work for her."

Other examples aren't hard to come by. Union Square Hospitality Group, chosen as one of the original Small Giants (companies that chose to be great instead of big), lives by four "Family Values": excellence, hospitality, entrepreneurial spirit, and integrity. Southwest Airlines, with a full-time culture director and more than 50,000 employees, has four company values: warrior spirit, servant's heart, fun-LUVing attitude, and work the Southwest way.

In each of these examples, the values are drastically different. Yet, if values are instilled in the culture, they capture the essence of a company's way of living and represent the most effective way to engage employees.

More companies should take time to live and breathe company values. When values are written down and discussed openly and consistently, all employees can better engage in the company's future.

CHAPTER 33

How to Lead vs. Manage Your Team's Success

by Bob Glazer

I t takes great leaders and talent to grow a successful company. One of the best descriptions of a leader I've heard is that leaders focus on vision and strategy, guiding and removing obstacles for their teams—something like a coach in sports.

Managers typically focus more on the execution piece: working in the business. By contrast, real leadership means providing a compelling vision and clear direction. Successful leaders clarify priorities and expectations, defining employee roles and ensuring that the processes and capacities required for them to execute are in place.

The stance from which you lead makes a big difference in your employees' job satisfaction. To engage your workers today, focus more on leading instead of managing. I've found that most employees are looking for coaches who can help them add value to the company by developing and making the most of their strengths. This is especially true when it comes to millennials, the largest generation in the work force.

Leading a productive team entails letting go of daily operations to focus on setting a clear strategy and vision—the "why" and "what"—and getting comfortable leaving your team to manage the "how." This can be a serious challenge if you're accustomed to spending most of your time triaging problems, putting out fires, and managing from a reactive standpoint.

Managers execute—leaders lead.

As the CEO of a digital marketing agency, I used to review every monthly report for quality before it went out to our clients, which involved far too much "managing" time.

Realizing it would not scale, I sat down one day and wrote a playbook on how to create these reports, trained the team, and then let them loose. I still ask to be copied on them, but now, I can focus on coaching people on opportunities to improve, and they know they won't get my feedback before they send. This approach creates more accountability for others and less doing on my part.

When I empowered the team to write those monthly reports, everyone saw better outcomes. Here are three more ways you can shift from day-to-day management to leadership.

1. Establish Core Values—and Follow Them

While 80 percent of Fortune 100 companies talk about their core values publicly, according to one study, they are often hollow words that aren't operationalized in any way. The magic of core values is that, when they are ingrained into employees' daily work lives, they drive more autonomous decision making.

For example, one of our core values is "embrace relationships," which empowers our managers to make financial decisions aligned with long-term outcomes—not short-term maximization of profits. Someone might say to me, "I made this concession for one of our partners because it was the right thing to do," rather than feel the need to ask for permission.

To create the right conditions for success and to lead by example, employees need to understand where the business is going and how they should behave. Your core values inform your company culture; including the team in creating those values can help workers feel more connected and empowered.

2. Don't Neglect Your Own Professional Development

Too often leaders assume responsibility for everyone on their teams but themselves. Although we all need to manage at times, leaders are usually proactive; managers are reactive. If you want to be a great leader, set aside time for your own professional development.

Join local and national professional organizations, such as Entrepreneurs' Organization—a great resource for networking and leadership training—or attend conferences such as GrowCo to hear from other leaders who have found success.

Look for groups that will challenge and support you in your professional development beyond networking and handing out business cards. Seek out a successful coach or mentor and create a formal board of advisors. Nothing is ever as easy as it looks, so lean on the support and experience of others to guide you and learn from those who have done what you aim to do.

And don't forget to transfer this focus on development to your team. GitHub, a code hosting provider for techies, for example, allows each of its employees to attend one work-related conference a year and covers the travel costs if a teammate is invited to speak.

3. Spread the Love, or Risk Burnout

If you try to do it all yourself, you will inevitably see diminishing returns on the time you invest. Successful leaders spend the majority of their time on tasks that use their own unique skills and abilities and leave the rest to others who are more competent in those areas.

Try this exercise to figure out how to make that happen:

- Determine the maximum number of hours per week you can work and stay balanced.
- Calculate (honestly) how much time it takes to do all your necessary tasks well. If the answer is more than 100 percent of your max hours, delegate.
- List everything you do in a day.
- Create two columns to sort that list: in column one, list every task you love to do and are great at; column two is for everything else.
- Stop doing, or delegate, everything in column two that puts you over capacity.

The great thing is you'll often discover that the duties you aren't good at (or don't enjoy) align with the unique capabilities and favorite tasks of someone else on your team.

Although it might seem impossible to let go of the daily tasks of managing the business, getting out of that mindset and focusing on how to be an inspirational leader is the best investment you can make in both your quality of life and the success of your business.

Index